ADVANCED EAR-TRAINING
and
SIGHT-SINGING

AS APPLIED TO THE
STUDY OF HARMONY

A Continuation of the
Practical and Coördinated Course for
Schools and Private Study

By

GEORGE A. WEDGE

G. SCHIRMER, Inc., NEW YORK

Printed in the U. S. A.

To
Dr. FRANK· DAMROSCH

PREFACE

The study of Harmony generally consists of writing notes, mathematically calculated from a figured bass, without hearing their sound or understanding their use and bearing upon playing or singing. A musician must be able to read and hear written music as readily as he reads his mother tongue.

The purpose of this book is to show the pupil how to study and apply Harmony, to develop the ability to hear what is written and to furnish exercises for study.

Each Lesson is divided into three Sections: Section A contains the exercises for written work, applying Harmony to Melodic Construction and Harmonization, and the study of Form; Section B, the exercises for Harmonic, Interval and Melodic Dictation; Section C, the exercises in Singing Intervals, Rhythms, Chords and Sight-Reading.

In class-work it has been found practical to use two fifty-minute periods a week, devoting one period to Sections A and B and the other to Section C. The explanations at the beginning of each Lesson combined with Section C can be used for the study of Sight-Singing without the written work of Section A and the Ear-Training of Section B.

Following is a plan of the book, showing the development of the work and order in which the factors are taken up.

AN ACKNOWLEDGMENT

The author wishes to express his gratitude to Dr. Frank Damrosch, who has encouraged and sponsored this work as it has been developed in the classes at the Institute of Musical Art;

To Miss Helen W. Whiley for loyalty and enthusiasm in presenting this material, and help in the preparation of the manuscript;

To Dr. Thomas Tapper for reviewing the manuscript;

To Dr. Percy Goetchius' "Tone Relations" and "Material Used in Musical Composition";

To Mr. Franklin W. Robinson for ideas in presenting Harmonic Dictation and the use and meaning of chords.

To G. Schirmer, Inc. for the use of copyrighted material in the Exercises for Sight-Singing.

GEORGE A. WEDGE.

North Brooklin, Maine,
August 15th, 1922.

CONTENTS

ADVANCED EAR-TRAINING AND SIGHT-SINGING

CHAPTER I

TRIADS

A *Chord* is a combination of three, four or five tones placed one above the

other in *thirds:* The tone upon which the chord is built is called the *Root.*

The next tone is the *third*, the next the *fifth*, the next the *seventh*, the next the *ninth of the chord.* Each tone is named from its interval-relationship to the root of the chord.

A three-tone chord is a *Triad:* A four-tone chord is a *Chord of the Seventh* (seventh-chord): A five-tone chord is a *Chord of the Ninth* (ninth-chord):

A chord may be built upon each tone of a key.

A chord is named from the degree of the scale which is its root. If the root is the first degree of the scale, it is a *One Chord* (I), or *Tonic Chord;* if the fifth degree, a *Five Chord* (V), or *Dominant Chord;* etc.

I V II IV VI III VII V⁷

Roman numerals are used as symbols of chords.

In triads, there is a duplication one octave higher of one of the tones, generally the root. The tonic chord is 1, 3, 5, 8; the dominant chord 5, 7, 2, 5; the sub-dominant chord 4, 6, 8, 4; the two chord 2, 4, 6, 2; the six chord 6, 8, 3, 6; the three chord 3, 5, 7, 3.

The I, V and IV chords consist of a major third and a perfect fifth from the root. These chords are *major chords.* The II, VI and III chords consist of a minor third and a perfect fifth from the root. These chords are *minor chords.* The VII chord consists of a minor third and a diminished fifth from the root. As this chord upon the leading tone is imperfect, i.e., the only chord with a diminished fifth, and is included in and used as the seventh-chord built upon the dominant, it is not considered, by most theorists, as an independent triad.

A chord is major or minor according to the size of its third.

Chords are arranged in harmony for four-part vocal music. The upper part is the *Soprano*, the next the *Alto.* These are written on the G staff. The next voice-part is the *Tenor* and the next the *Bass.* These are written on the F staff.

A chord is in *octave position* when the 8th of the chord is in the soprano. It is in *the position of the 5th* when the fifth of the chord is in the soprano. It is in *the position of the 3rd* when the third of the chord is in the soprano.   The *root* is in the bass.   The position of a chord has nothing to do with Inversion, which will be treated later.

Chords are used in music to establish the key and to give accent.   The progression or resolution of one chord into another produces an accent.   Therefore, the chord on the unaccented pulse resolves into the chord on the accented pulse.

Chords are built upon the tones of the key, i.e., the different tones found by dividing a string into thirds, and not upon these pitches arranged in the major scale relationship.   Chords are related to and progress to the I chord as these tones are related to the key-tone.   If C is the key-tone, the tones of the

key are:

These tones as roots of chords and arranged in this order are:

VII
III
VI
II
V
I
IV

The only tone in this series which is at rest is the key-tone.   The other tones are active in their relationship with C.   In arranging the chords the IV is transposed and placed between the II and the VI, as the II⁷ chord includes the IV

and is nearer the key-centre.

Compositions generally begin with the I chord and may progress to any chord.   As all other chords are active, they will have to progress to more active chords until they come to rest on the I chord.   For example, if we progress from the I to the VI, the VI will progress to some other chord nearer the centre, the IV, II or V, and then to the I.

The V and IV chords are the only chords which may progress immediately to the I.   The other chords will pass through V or IV before going to I.   The III always goes to IV or II before going to V.

This law of the progression of the roots of chords is known as the *Harmonic Law* and the progression from one tone to the next in this series an *Harmonic Step* or *Degree*.

The three upper voices of chords resolve according to the law of active and rest tones in the major scale which is the *Melodic Law*.   It will be found that if the root of the chord fulfills the harmonic law the three upper voices will fulfill the melodic law.

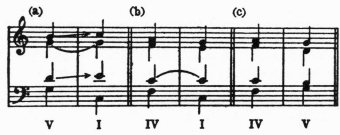

When the V chord progresses to the I chord as in (a) the root V in the bass progresses an harmonic step to the I; the 7th degree in the soprano progresses to the 8th; the 5th degree, which is a rest tone, remains stationary; the 2nd degree progresses to the 3rd.

In the progression IV to I, as in (b), the root IV in the bass goes to the I; the 6th degree in the soprano to the 5th; the 4th degree to the 3rd; the 1st degree remains at rest.

In the progression IV to V, the root of the IV progresses harmonically to the root of the V; the 6th degree in the soprano moves to the 5th; the 4th degree, which must resolve down, moves to the 2nd, as there is no 3rd degree in the V chord; the 8th degree moves to the 7th.

Lesson 1.

Section A.

(1)   Learn the arrangement of the chord roots in the harmonic series.

(2)   Construct melodies, phrases in length, in 6/8 meter, using the I, V and IV chords as a basis for the melody.   Employ any of the following rhythms:

In writing a melody, using chords as a basis, first divide the staff into measures and place the chord symbols underneath, one chord for each pulse.

The choice of chords is determined by the harmonic law.

A chord may be repeated within a measure, but not over the bar.

A phrase when regular will begin with the I chord on the accented or un-accented pulse and will end with the I chord on an accented pulse of the fourth measure, preceded by the V chord.   This is an *Authentic Cadence*.   If the final I chord is in the position of the octave, a *Perfect Authentic Cadence* results; if in the position of the third or fifth, the cadence is known as *Imperfect Authentic*.   A phrase generally ends with a Perfect Authentic Cadence.

A melody may follow the line of a scale up or down.   In working from an harmonic basis the melody will **move** along the scale-line from some tone of the chord on the pulse.   Not all the tones of the scale will be found in this chord. The tones which come between the tones of the chord are called *Passing-Tones*, and do not affect the harmony.

At any time the melody may stop and embellish a tone of the chord by pro-gressing to the tone a half-step or whole step above or below.   These tones are known as *Neighboring Tones*, and do not affect the harmony.   Neighboring tones must always return to the principal tone and may never jump, unless from the upper to the lower neighbor or the reverse.

All skips, single or consecutive, must occur between tones of the chord. Occasionally a skip may be made to a neighbor; the neighbor must immediately resolve to the principal tone.

For example, divide the staff into four measures.   As these melodies are to be in 6/8 meter, we shall have two chords in each measure but the last.   The phrase may end on the first or second pulse of the fourth measure as it is a compound meter.   On the first pulse we may have a I chord and repeat it for the second; on the third the V and its resolution on the fourth; then the IV, which may go either to the V or I.   In the following example the IV will move to the V on account of the cadence.

I   I   V   I   IV   V   I

The melody may start with 8 and progress down the scale to 3, making b, a and f, passing-tones; then to 2, a part of the V chord on the next pulse; then to 1, the lower neighbor of 2, and back to 2; then to 3 for the I chord, passing through 4 and 5 to 6 for the IV chord; then skip in the IV chord from 6 to 4 to 8; turning after the wide skip to 7, a member of the V chord, and passing through 8 up to 2 and returning to 8 for the cadence.

Section B.

(1) Play the following chord successions, listening to the difference in sound of the I and V chords. The I chord gives a feeling of rest, because the root is the fundamental tone in the harmonic series and the three upper voices are rest tones of the major scale. If the I chord is in octave position, it sounds complete; if it is in the position of the third or fifth it gives a feeling of rest, but sounds incomplete or questioning.

The V chord sounds unfinished and as if the I chord should follow. It is an active chord and needs resolution into the I chord, because its root is the nearest related tone to the I chord in the harmonic series and two of its upper voices are active tones in the major scale and demand resolution.

In listening to the chord, hear it as a complex of tones, if it is at rest or needs resolution, do not listen primarily to the bass or soprano. In chord repetitions the same sounds will be heard, but in different arrangement.

Practise as follows:

(a) Play each exercise several times, determining if the chords are active or at rest.

(b) After each V chord pause for a moment so that the mind may realize the demand for resolution.

(c) Play the first chord and think the sound of the others. Test with the piano to see if you think correctly.

(d) Use each exercise for dictation as follows:

(1) Rule the staff for four measures.

(2) Have someone play the exercise slowly, twice.

(3) At the second playing write the chord symbols according as you think it is the I or the V chord.

(4) Have the exercise played again and write the numbers of the scale steps in the soprano.

(5) Compare your version with the exercise. If there is a mistake, play your version, then the correct chord, until you hear the mistake.

Exercise *a* would be written:

The chords of this exercise will be heard thus: The first chord as the I, the next a different chord demanding resolution into the I, so it must be the V; the next the I, as the resolution of the V; the next as the same chord, the position having been changed; the next a different chord and an active chord; the next the same chord in a different position; the last the I, as the resolution of the V.

(2) An Harmonic and most Melodic Intervals are parts of a chord *and sound in relation* to the root of the chord.

All the intervals in the I chord are consonant intervals, or intervals which do not need resolution.

The Major 3rd, 1–3, from the Root to the Third of the chord.

The Minor 3rd, 3–5, from the Third to the Fifth of the chord.

The Major 6th, 5–3, from the Fifth to the Third of the chord.

The Minor 6th, 3–8, from the Third to the Eighth of the chord.

The Perfect 5th, 1–5, from the Root to the Fifth of the chord.

The Perfect 4th, 5–8, from the Fifth to the Eighth of the chord.

Since the I, V and IV chords are major chords, their interval content is the same.

As these chords are used in composition, the same intervals occur between different scale-degrees.

In the V, or Dominant Chord:
  Major 3rd, Root to Third, from
    5th–7th degree
  Minor 3rd, Third to Fifth, from
    7th–2nd degree

In the IV, or Subdominant Chord:
  from the 4th–6th degree

  from the 6th–8th degree

Major 6th, Fifth to Third, from 2nd – 7th degree	from the 1st – 6th degree
Minor 6th, Third to Eighth, from 7th – 5th degree	from the 6th – 4th degree
Perfect 5th, Root to Fifth, from 5th – 2nd degree	from the 4th – 8th degree
Perfect 4th, Fifth to Eighth, from 2nd – 5th degree	from the 1st – 4th degree

All these intervals are consonant and are therefore complete, requiring no resolution; as they occur in the I chord there is no question as to their position in the key. As different chords are used and four or five intervals occur in a chord, other than the I chord, there is a danger, because of their consonant quality, of losing the feeling of active and inactive scale-degrees or of the key-centre. This cannot happen if the change of chord is recognized and the position of the intervals in the chord is known. For example, in this series the first three intervals, a major 3rd, 1 – 3, a perfect 5th, 1 – 5, a minor 6th, 3 – 8, are known to be in the I chord, as music generally begins with the I chord.

The next interval might be heard in the following ways:
  (a) As a major 3rd, but not in the I chord. If the new chord is recognized as the V chord, its position is known to be from the 5th to the 7th degree of the scale.
  (b) If the scale-degrees 5 and 7 are recognized, it is known to be a major 3rd and a part of the V chord.
  (c) The 7th degree might be recognized as the upper tone of a major 3rd, so the interval is from the 5th to the 7th degree and a part of the V chord.

The next interval might be heard:
  (a) As a perfect 5th and in the same chord as the preceding interval, therefore from the 5th to the 2nd degree.
  (b) If the scale-degrees 5 and 2 are heard, it is known to be a perfect 5th in the V chord.
  (c) It is more likely to sound 1 to 5, or Root to Fifth. This interval is felt to be a part of the same chord as the preceding interval, so it could not be from the 1st degree to the 5th, but from the Root to the Fifth of the V chord, and from the 5th to the 2nd degree.

The next interval, a perfect 4th, will undoubtedly sound like 5 up to 1; the next, a minor 6th, 3 up to 8. Unless we realize that these intervals are in the same chord as the two preceding and sound in relation to the root of that chord, the key-centre is lost. If they are known to be a perfect 4th, from the 5th to the 1st (or Root), and a minor 6th, from the 3rd to the 8th of the V chord (not of the scale), they are easily placed in the key.

The last interval is heard as a major 3rd in a different chord. As only the I chord may follow the V chord, the interval must be from 1 to 3.

Practise the following:

(a) Play the I, IV and V chords in the key of C. Think the sound of the intervals. Test with the piano. The intervals in Exercises 1 and 2 are in the I and V chords; in Ex. 3, 4, 5 and 6, in the I, IV and V chords.

(b) Play the intervals, listening to determine how they sound in relation to the root of the chord and to the key-centre.

(c) Play the lower tone, sing the upper tone of each.
     Play the upper tone, sing the lower tone of each.

(3) *Exercises for Melodic Dictation and Sight-Singing.*

Practise:

(a) Play the I, V and I chords in C major to establish the tonality.

(b) Read the melody mentally, without singing, at a moderate tempo. M M ♩. = 72. Test with the piano. If you cannot hear the melody mentally, play the melody, then try to read it mentally. It is most vital that written music should be read and heard mentally as readily as one reads English.

If this is at first difficult, persist: it is the greatest aid to sight-singing.

(c) Play the phrase twice, look away from the music and sing the phrase from memory to *la*. Test. Repeat until successful.

Sing from memory, using the number-names of the scale-degrees; then use the letter-names.

(d) Play the I, V and I chords in D Major. Sing the melody, using first the number, then the letter-names. Transpose the melody to B Major in the same way.

NOTE. Let the construction of the melody help in memorizing. In 2 the first four notes form a figure, the next four are in a sequence with it: the next measure is a scale-line on the first pulse and a wide leap on the second.

In singing and memorizing a melody beginning on the up-beat, be sure that the measure is felt from the up-beat to the up-beat.

(e) Have someone play the melodies for dictation as follows:

(1) Play the entire melody with simple chord accompaniment, two chords to a measure, using the I, IV and V chords on the pulses, allowing the other tones to be passing-tones or neighbors. Number 1 would be harmonized:

The pupil decides the meter and form of the melody. The *form* is determined by the cadence; the *meter* by the number of pulses in the phrase.

(2) Play the phrase twice while the pupil listens and memorizes the tune. The pupil should relax and allow the entire phrase to make an impression on the mind; he should not spend time

trying to determine the note it begins on or analyzing a rhythmic complication. After the mind has grasped the phrase it is easily analyzed. As these phrases are in compound meter, remember that a mental breath in the middle of the phrase will help in memorizing.

(3) The pupil writes the melody on the staff. At this stage there should be no difficulty in writing, but if there is, make an outline as in the elementary work.

If the pupil has trouble with the rhythm in only one measure, write dots for the pulses and determine the figure on each pulse.

(4) Play the phrase again for correction.

(5) After the melody is written, the pupil should mark the chords that may be used for harmonizing the melody, as well as the rhythmic figures, sequences and repetitions.

The chord symbols indicate the harmonic background. The question of inversions to avoid parallel fifths and octaves is left until those points are taken up in the theoretic study.

Section C.

(1) *Absolute Intervals.*

In sight-singing there is no need of thinking the interval name or the size of the skip made, as long as the key is known. It is only when this feeling of key has been broken down by unusual skips or a modulation that a knowledge of how to sing absolute or unrelated intervals is needed, and then only until the tonality has been reëstablished. The position of intervals on the staff and in the major scale, also of what chords they are a part, must be known so that they may be quickly recognized and sung.

There are major 3rds on the staff from c–e, f–a, g–b; in the major scale from 1-3, 4-6, 5-7; in the I, V, II, IV, VI and III chords.

To sing a major 3rd up, make the lower tone 1 and sing 3; to sing a major 3rd down, make the upper tone 3 and sing 1.

(a) Play any tone on the piano, sing the tone calling it 1, then sing the tone a major 3rd above, calling it 3. Test.

(b) Play any tone on the piano, sing the tone calling it 3, then sing the tone a major 3rd below, calling it 1.

(c) Repeat, singing the letter-names of the pitches.

(2) *Rhythmic Study:* ♪.♫♫ **in** ⅝

As 6/8 is a Duple Metre, each pulse divided into triplets, beat two to a measure and intone the rhythms. The rhythmic subdivision must be felt and sung as a unit. In singing any rhythmic subdivision there is a feeling of relaxation

after the tone on the pulse, e.g.,  In each

of these figures there is a feeling of stress on the first tone and relaxation for the other tones. Each group should be mentally conceived as a figure before singing, the eye taking in as a unit the figure on each pulse and not each individual note. It has been found practical in studying these exercises to sing a major scale as well as intoning the rhythm on one pitch. Begin on 8 and sing down; (a) would be sung:

The figure ♪.♫♫ is often confused with ♪ ♫. This is easily corrected,

as the two sixteenths in the figure ♪ ♫ relate themselves to and progress

into the next pulse. The figure ♪.♫♫ halts and is not legato.

Rhythmic Study contrasting ♪.♫♫ *and* ♪ ♫.

(3)   *The following Chord Successions are to be practised:*
   (a)   Play the key-tone. Think, or hear mentally, the exercise in a moderate tempo.
   (b)   Sing the chords, using the letter-names, c, e, g, c, etc. Sing the numbers of the scale-steps, 1, 3, 5, 8, etc.
   (c)   Write the chord symbols I, V, I, IV, I and sing the letter- and number-names from memory.
   (d)   Test at the end of each exercise to see if you are singing on pitch. If below pitch, repeat more slowly, taking care that the 5th and 8th of each chord are high enough.
   (e)   Sing each chord as follows: Root, 3rd, 5th, 8th, 5th, 3rd, Root.
   (f)   Sing the exercise to a neutral syllable, as *la*, thinking first the letter, then the number-names.
   (g)   Repeat each exercise until it can be sung rhythmically.

(4)   *Exercises for Sight-Singing:*
    (a)   Play the I, V and I chords to establish the tonality.
    (b)   Read the exercise through mentally at a moderately slow tempo. Test for pitch.
    (c)   Sing the exercise to the number-names of the scale-steps; to the letter-names of the pitches.
    (d)   Sing to the syllable *la*, thinking first the number-names, then the letter-names.

NOTE. Beat two beats to the measure. Take in each pulse as a unit. In consecutive leaps, think the sound of the entire chord.

LESSON 2

A phrase in music corresponds to a simple sentence in English. In English a compound sentence is often used; this is, in reality, two sentences, each expressing a complete thought, the one qualifying the other. In music a *Period* corresponds to this form.

A Period, when regular, consists of two phrases, each usually four measures long. The first is the *Antecedent Phrase*, the second the *Consequent Phrase*. A period begins as any phrase, but the antecedent phrase ends with some tone of the V chord, 5, 7 or 2. This gives the effect of being incomplete and makes a *Semi-cadence*. The consequent phrase ends with the 1 or 8, a Perfect Authentic Cadence.

A period is in *Parallel Construction* when at least the first measure of the antecedent and that of the consequent phrase are alike, as Melody 3, Section B (3). (Page 18.)

A period is in *Contrasting Construction* when the antecedent and consequent phrases are different, as Melody 2, Section B (3).

Melodies are constructed in the Minor Mode the same as in the Major Mode, the Minor Mode being formed from the Major by lowering the 3rd and 6th degrees of the Major.

In using the progression from the 6th to the 7th degrees, the augmented 2nd, which sounds like a minor 3rd, is often retained,  but generally in ascending the 6th degree is raised and in descending the 7th degree is lowered so as to give a diatonic progression. This is known as the Melodic Minor Scale and is used when the scale-line is harmonized with the I chord.

I   I   IV   I

If the harmony is the V chord, the raised 6th is used both in ascending and descending.

V   V   I

If the harmony is the IV, II or VI chord, the lowered 7th is used both in ascending and descending.

VI   IV   II   V

Section A.

(1) Construct periods in c minor, with both parallel and contrasting phrases, using the I, V and IV chords as a basis for the melody. Employ the following rhythms in 6/8 meter: ♩. ; ♩ ♪ ; ♪♪♪ ; ♩ ♪♪ ; ♪♪♪♪♪♪ ; ♪.♪♪ .

Section B.

(1) Play the following chord successions, listening to the difference in sound of the I and V chords in minor. The I is a rest chord as in major, but is minor in quality on account of the lowered 3rd degree. The V chord is active, is major in quality, and sounds the same in the major and minor modes.

Practise 1, 2, *and* 3, *as follows:*
- (a) Play each exercise several times, determining if the chords are active or at rest.
- (b) After each V chord pause for a minute and think the chord of resolution before playing it.
- (c) Play the first chord and think the sound of the others. Test with the piano.
- (d) Have each exercise dictated. Work as outlined on page 4.
- (e) Transpose the exercises of Lesson 1 *to c minor.*

In Exercises 4, 5, 6, 7 and 8, in C major, the IV chord is used. The IV chord is major in sound, and is an active chord because its root is the first harmonic tone below the Tonic and two of its upper voices are active tones in the melodic series. The IV chord resolves into the I, or it may progress into the V. It is distinguishable from the V chord because it sounds lower and farther from the I; it impresses the ear as if another chord could be played before its resolution into the I. It is impossible to think a chord between the V and I.

Practise these Exercises as follows:
- (a) Play each exercise, determining if the chords are active or at rest.
- (b) Pause after each V chord and think the chord of resolution.
- (c) Pause after each IV chord and think first the I chord, then the V and I chords.
- (d) Think the sound of each exercise.
- (e) Have the exercises dictated.

Ex. 5 would be heard: first a I chord; next an active chord, before the resolution of which another active chord could be substituted; or as an active chord resolving into the I and sounding like an "A-men," therefore the IV-I; the next a rest chord, the I: the next the same chord in another position; the next an active chord resolving to another active chord, which must be the IV to the V chord; the next the rest chord.

- (f) Transpose each exercise to c minor.

In minor the IV chord is a minor chord and is distinguished from the I chord, which is also minor, on account of its activity.

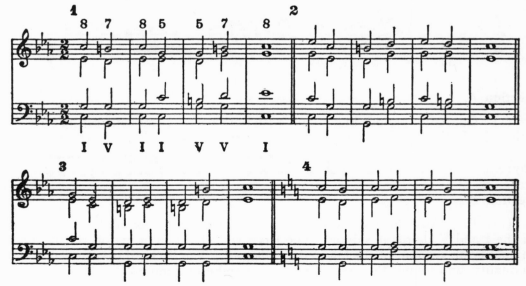

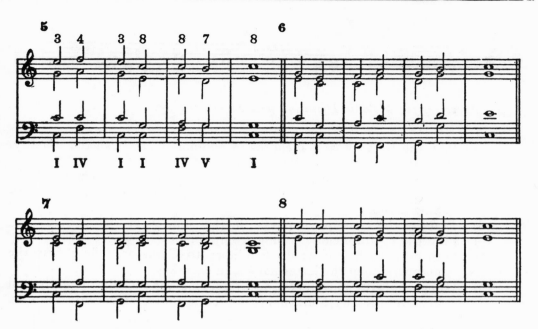

(2) In minor the position of the major and minor intervals in the I and IV chords will be changed on account of the lowering of the 3rd and 6th degrees of the scale. The minor 3rd will occur from the root to the 3rd of the chord; the major 3rd from the 3rd to the 5th of the chord; the major 6th from the 3rd to the 8th of the chord; the minor 6th from the 5th to the 3rd of the chord. The perfect intervals will remain the same. The intervals in the V chord will not change.

Practise the following:
  (a) Play the I, IV and V chords in c minor. Think the sound of the intervals. Test with the piano.
  (b) Play the intervals, listening to determine how they sound in relation to the root of the chord and to the key-centre.
  (c) Play the lower tone, sing the upper tone of each.
        Play the upper tone, sing the lower tone of each.

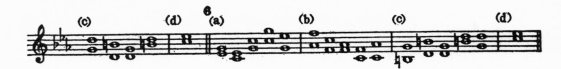

(3)   *Exercises for Melodic Dictation and Sight-Singing.*

Practise:
  (a)   Play the I, IV, V and I chords in c minor to establish the tonality.
  (b)   Read the melody mentally.   Test.
  (c)   Play the antecedent phrase twice.   Sing it from memory to *la*. Sing mentally the number-names; then use the letter-names. Sing aloud.
  (d)   Practise the consequent phrase in the same way.
  (e)   Play the entire melody.   Sing from memory.
  (f)   Transpose to d minor; to b minor; to C major.   Sing first the number-, then the letter-names, in each key.
  (g)   Using the arm movement, down-up, sing the melody mentally and analyse the rhythmic figure on each pulse.   Concentrate upon the figures of three notes to the pulse, ♪♪♪ , ♩ ♫ , and ♩.♪♪ .   If there is confusion of ♩ ♫ and ♩.♪♪ , substitute one for the other until the difference is felt.   Review "Rhythmic Drill," page 10.

(h) Have each melody dictated as follows:

(1) Play the entire period with simple accompaniment, two chords to a measure, using the I, IV and V chords on the pulses, allowing the other tones to be passing-tones or neighbors. The pupil decides the form, the construction, if parallel or contrasting, and the meter.

(2) Play the antecedent phrase twice while the pupil listens and memorizes the tune. Do not allow the pupil to sing the melody aloud. He should sing mentally.

(3) The pupil analyses and writes the melody on the staff.

(4) Play the phrase again for correction.

(5) Dictate the consequent phrase in the same manner.

(6) The pupil marks the chords for harmonization, the figures, repetitions and sequences and the form of the melody.

Section C.

(1) *Absolute Intervals.*

There are minor 3rds on the staff from d–f, e–g, a–c, b–d; in the major scale from 2–4, 3–5, 6–8, 7–2; in the I, V, II, IV, VI and III chords. To sing a minor 3rd up, call the lower tone 3 and sing 5; to sing a minor 3rd down, call the upper tone 5 and sing 3.

>   (a)   Play any tone on the piano; sing the tone, calling it 3; then sing the tone a minor 3rd above, calling it 5.   Test.
>   (b)   Play any tone on the piano; sing the tone, calling it 5; then sing the tone a minor third below, calling it 3.
>   (c)   Repeat, singing the letter-names of the pitches.

(2)   *Rhythmic Study:*

The three sixteenths in the figure ![figure] group themselves with the next pulse, the same as the two sixteenths in the figure ![figure].   Study using the arm movement for the pulse and singing each exercise to *la* on a major scale, as in the preceding Lesson.   These exercises should be sung at a moderate tempo, about ♩. =69, gradually increasing to about ♩. =88.   In all of the drill both for Rhythm and in Sight-Singing use a light tone so that there is no concern about tone-production.

>   (3)   *Practise the following Chord Successions:*
>   (a)   Play the key-tone and sing the exercise mentally.
>   (b)   Sing, using the letter-names.   Sing, using the number-names.
>   (c)   Sing to *la*, thinking the letter-names, then the number-names.
>   (d)   Write out the chord symbols and sing the letter- and number-names from memory.   In singing from memory, always have a mental picture of the staff or look at a blank staff.

NOTE.   In exercises 3 and 4, where the descending arpeggio is rapid, it must be thought of as a unit 8531, not each tone 8, 5, 3, 1.   To do this the mind must relax after the note on the pulse.

(4) *Exercises for Sight-Singing:*
  (a) Play the I, IV, V and I chords and read each exercise through
       mentally.   Test for pitch.
  (b) Sing each exercise to the number-names of the scale-steps; to the
       letter-names of the pitches.
  (c) Sing to the syllable *la*, thinking first the number-names, then the
       letter-names.
Note the skips in the IV chord.

LESSON 3

The II chord is minor in quality and is next to the V chord in activity. It is called the Second Dominant Chord because its root is the second dominant from the tonic in the Harmonic Series.

The II chord may be preceded by any chord but the V. It resolves into the V chord. Exceptionally it may resolve into the VI chord, as will be explained later under "Exceptional Resolutions," in Lesson 4, page 33.

Section A.

(1) Construct periods in G major, with both parallel and contrasting phrases, using the I, V, IV and II chords as a basis for the melody. Employ the following rhythms in 6/8 meter:

Section B.

(1) *Practise the following Chord Successions:*
    (a) Play each exercise several times, determining if the chords are active or at rest, major or minor.
    (b) Pause after each active chord and think its resolution.
    (c) Read each exercise mentally.
    (d) Have each exercise dictated. Work as outlined on page 4.

The II chord will be heard as a minor chord. At first it will be confused with the IV chord. Always go back and substitute the IV for the II if this mistake is made, determining if the quality of the chord is major or minor. Remember that a chord is not repeated over the bar.

(2) The minor 3rd and perfect 5th in the II chord, are from the root to the 3rd and the root to the 5th of the chord: from the 2nd to the 4th and the 2nd to the 6th degrees of the scale. The intervals in the II chord will follow the intervals in the IV chord, and will be followed by intervals in the V chord.

Practise the following:

   (a) Play the I, IV, II, V and I chords in G major. Think the sound of the intervals. Test with the piano.

   (b) Play the intervals, listening to determine how they sound in relation to the root of the chord and to the key-centre.

   (c) Play the lower tone, sing the upper tone of each.
        Play the upper tone, sing the lower tone of each.

(3) *Exercises for Melodic Dictation and Sight-Singing*, containing skips in

the II chord and employing the rhythmic figure [♩. ♫♫] in 6/8 meter.

Practise:

(a) Play the I, IV, II, V and I chords in G major.

(b) Read the melody mentally. Test.

(c) Play the antecedent phrase twice. Sing from memory to *la*. Sing mentally the number-names; then use the letter-names. Sing aloud.

(d) Practise the consequent phrase in the same way.

(e) Play the entire melody. Sing from memory. Use the period-form, figures, repetitions and sequences, as an aid to memorizing.

(f) Use the arm movement for beating the meter and mentally analyse the rhythmic figures.

(g) Transpose to F and A major, singing the number- and letter names.

(h) Have each melody dictated as outlined on page 19.

Section C.

(1) *Absolute Intervals.*

All of the 4ths on the staff are perfect, except f–b; in the major scale, except 4–7; in the minor scale, all but 4–7, 6–2, 7–3.   To sing a perfect 4th up, call the lower tone 5 and sing 8; to sing a perfect 4th down, call the upper tone 8 and sing 5.

> (a)   Play any tone on the piano; sing the tone, calling it 5; then sing the tone a perfect 4th above, calling it 8.   Test.
>
> (b)   Play any tone on the piano;   sing the tone, calling it 8; then sing the tone a perfect 4th below, calling it 5.   Test.
>
> (c)   Repeat, singing the letter-names of the pitches.

(2) *Rhythmic Study:*

> (a)   Study using the arm movement to indicate the meter, and sing the rhythms to *la* in a major scale.

(3) *Practise the following Chord Successions:*
(a)   Play the key-tone and sing the exercises mentally.
(b)   Sing using the letter-names; the number-names.
(c)   Sing to *la*, thinking the letter-names; the number-names.
(d)   Sing from memory.

Sing the following chord succession in the same rhythm as 2: I, II, V, IV, V, 1
Sing the following in the same rhythms as 3: I, IV, I, IV, II, V, I. Test fo
pitch at the end of each exercise, even the mental exercises, so as to be sure
that you are thinking and singing in tune. If below pitch at the end of the exercise, repeat, testing after each chord. The flatting is generally caused by not
placing the 8th of the chord high enough. Use the piano only to test. Do not
play as you sing. Learn to think in tune.

(4) *Exercises for Sight-Singing:*
    (a) Play the I, IV, II, V and I chords, and read each exercise mentally.
        Test for pitch.
    (b) Sing each exercise to the number-names; to the letter-names.
    (c) Sing to the syllable *la*, thinking first the number-names, then the
        letter-names.

Note the skips in the II chord. Recognize the chord as a tone group, and
sing all of the notes on one pulse as a unit.

LESSON 4

The VI chord is minor in quality. It is preceded by the I chord and may be followed by any chord but the I. In the harmonic series the root normally progresses to the IV.

The III chord is a minor chord in quality. It is generally preceded by the I chord and is followed by the IV chord, as it is best used to harmonize the melodic progression 8 7 6 5.

I   III   IV   I

The following exceptions to the harmonic law are possible because the three upper voices resolve properly, fulfilling the melodic law, thus counteracting the exceptional resolution of the root of the chord.

The V chord may progress to the VI instead of the I chord. This progression is known as the *Deceptive Cadence*.

The II chord and the IV chord may also progress to the VI.

The following exceptions to the melodic law are possible because the roots of the chords are fulfilling the harmonic law.

The 4th degree of the scale may be forced up if harmonized with the IV chord resolving to the I chord or the II chord resolving to the V chord.

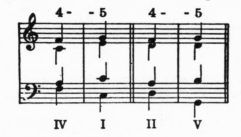

The 6th degree of the scale may be forced up if harmonized by the II chord progressing to the V chord.

The 7th degree of the scale may be forced down if harmonized with the III chord progressing to the IV chord.

Section A.

(1)   Construct periods in D major, with both parallel and contrasting phrases, using the I, V, II, IV, III and VI chords as a basis for the melody.   Employ the rhythms given on page 28.

Section B.

(1)   *Practise the following Chord Successions:*

    (a)   Play each exercise, determining if the chords are active or at rest, major or minor.

    (b)   Pause after each active chord and think its resolution.

    (c)   Pause after each minor chord and determine if it sounds like the I chord or the IV chord.

As both the II and the VI are minor chords, they are distinguishable by their relation to the IV and the I chords.   The II, having two tones in common with the IV chord, sounds like the IV; the VI, having two tones in common with the I chord, sounds like the I.

    (d)   Read the exercise mentally.

    (e)   Have each exercise dictated.   Work as outlined on page 4.

The position of the minor chord will often determine if it is a VI or a II; i.e., the VI would not follow the IV or the II follow the V.

(2)   The minor 3rd and perfect 5th in the VI chord are from root to the 3rd and the root to the 5th of the chord; from the 6th to the 8th and the 6th to the 3rd degrees of the scale.   The intervals in the VI chord will follow the intervals in the I chord and will be followed by intervals in any chord but the I chord.

Practise the following:
  (a)   Play the I, VI, IV, II, V and I chords in D major.   Think the sound of the the intervals.   Test with the piano.
  (b)   Play the intervals, listening to determine how they sound in relation to the root of the chord and to the key-centre.
  (c)   Play the lower tone, sing the upper.
        Play the upper tone, sing the lower.
  (d)   Transpose the intervals to the keys of C and G major.

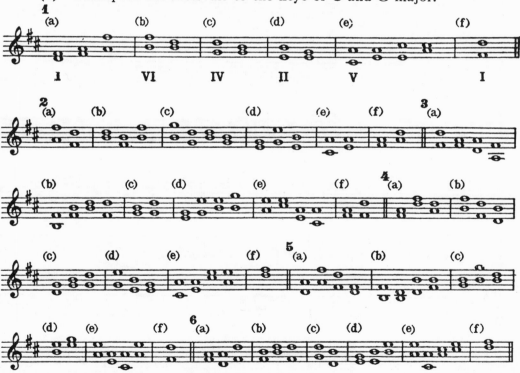

(3)   *Exercises for Melodic Dictation and Sight-Singing*, containing skips in the VI chord and employing the rhythmic figures ♩♫♩ , ♩♩♫ in 6/8 meter.

Practise:

    (a)   Play the I, VI, IV, II, V and I chords in D major.

    (b)   Read the melody mentally.   Test.

    (c)   Play the antecedent phrase twice.   Sing from memory to *la*.
           Sing mentally the number-names; then use the letter-names.
           Sing aloud.

    (d)   Practise the consequent phrase in the same way.

    (e)   Play the entire melody.   Sing from memory.

    (f)   Use the arm movement for beating the meter and mentally analyze
           the rhythmic figures.

    (g)   Transpose to E and C major, singing the number- and letter-names.

    (h)   Have each melody dictated as outlined on page 19.

There will be no difficulty in determining the pitches of the wide skips and consecutive skips if the chord in which the skips are made is recognized.   Apply the chords used in Section B (1).

Section C.

(1) *Absolute Intervals.*

All of the 5ths on the staff are perfect except b–f; in the major scale, except 7–4; in the minor scale, all except 7–4, 2–6, 3–7. To sing a perfect 5th up, call the lower tone 1 and sing 5; to sing a perfect 5th down, call the upper tone 5 and sing 1.

    (a)   Play any tone on the piano, sing the tone, calling it 1; then sing the tone a perfect fifth above, calling it 5. Test.

    (b)   Play any tone on the piano, sing the tone, calling it 5; then sing the tone a perfect 5th below, calling it 1. Test.

    (c)   Repeat, singing the letter-names of the pitches.

(2) *Rhythmic Study:* The Up-beat in 6/8.

    (a)   Study using the arm movement to indicate the meter, and sing the rhythms to *la* on a major scale.

Note that each of these phrases divides into two sections of two measures each, as indicated by the slurs. Remember that when the phrase begins on the accented pulse of the meter, the measure is from bar to bar. When the phrase begins on the up-beat, each measure begins on the up-beat. Ex. *e* divides as

Great care must be taken always to group the last two eighths in a measure with the following pulse:

(3)   *Practise the following Chord Successions:*

    (a)   Play the key-tone and sing the exercise mentally.

    (b)   Sing using the letter-names; then using the number-names.

    (c)   Sing to *la* thinking the letter-names; then think the number-names.

    (d)   Sing from the chord symbols without reference to the notes on the staff.

NOTE. The III chord is minor. It follows the I chord and resolves into the IV chord. It is little used except to harmonize the 7th degree of the scale as it progresses down to the 6th degree.

(e)   Sing the following chords in the rhythm of 1: I, IV, II, V, VI, V, I.
      Sing the following chords in the rhythm of 2: I, II, V, I, VI, IV, V, I.
      Sing the following chords in the rhythm of 3: I, VI, V, I, VI, IV, II, V, I.

(f)   Additional pitch drill. In the following exercises think, then sing, using letter- and number-names:
      (1)   Root of I chord, R of IV, R of V, 3rd of I, 3rd of V, 5th of V, R of I, 3rd of IV, 5th of IV, R of II, 5th of V, R of I.
      (2)   R of I, R of IV, 3rd of II, 5th of II, R of V, 3rd of V, R of I.
      (3)   5th of I, R of V, 5th of V, 3rd of I, 3rd of VI, R of VI, 5th of VI, R of II, 3rd of II, 3rd of V, R of I.

The chords should be seen mentally on the staff as these exercises are sung. If this is not possible at first, the chords may be written out in close position on the staff and referred to.

4.   *Exercises for Sight-Singing:*

CHAPTER II

INVERSIONS OF TRIADS

A chord is in *Fundamental Position* when its Root is in the bass.

A chord is *Inverted* when its 3rd, 5th or 7th is in the bass.

When a chord has its 3rd in the bass, it is in the *First Inversion*.

When a chord has its 5th in the bass, it is in the *Second Inversion*.

When a seventh-chord has its 7th in the bass, it is in the *Third Inversion*.

A small Arabic numeral placed to the right of the chord symbol indicates the inversion: I_1.

Chords are inverted so as to allow the bass to progress melodically along the diatonic scale.

LESSON 5

The first inversions of the I, IV and V chords are weaker than the fundamental positions.

The II chord is better and more easily handled in the first inversion.

A chord in the first inversion will progress to the chord an harmonic degree below, the same as when in fundamental position.

If there is a succession of chords in the first inversion, the bass and soprano will move in parallel 6ths. Because of this diatonic parallel motion the harmonic law will be ignored.

Section A.

(1) Construct periods in F major, with both parallel and contrasting phrases, using the I, VI, IV, II and V chords in fundamental position and first inversion as a basis for the melody. Employ the rhythmic figures given on page 37, 6/8 meter.

[43]

In constructing a melody when using the first inversion of a chord on a pulse, the 5th or the root of the chord will be used on the pulse, never the 3rd, if the chord is major.   The 3rd is possible when the chord is minor.

Section B.

(1)   *Practise the following Chord Successions:*
   (a)   Play each exercise, determining if the chords are active or at rest, major or minor, in fundamental position or inverted.
   (b)   Pause after each active chord and think its resolution; after each minor chord and think its major relative chord; after each first inversion and think the fundamental position.
   (c)   Read the exercise mentally.   Test with the piano to see if you think correctly.   If there is trouble in thinking a chord, play it several times, then go back until you can hear it.
   (d)   Have each exercise dictated.   Work as outlined on page 4.

The mind must attach some definite meaning to the sound of first inversions. The I_1, IV_1, V_1 all sound weaker than the fundamental position.   They also sound top-heavy.   They can be distinguished by the smooth progression into the next chord.   This is difficult and cannot be mastered in one lesson.   It is only by constant practice and drill that one comes definitely to hear inversions.

(2) *Practise the following Intervals:*
   (a) Play the I, VI, IV, II, V and I chords in F major. Think the sound of the intervals. Test.
   (b) Play the intervals, listening to determine how they sound in relation to the root of the chord and to the key-centre.
   (c) Play the lower tone, sing the upper.
         Play the upper tone, sing the lower.
   (d) Transpose the intervals to the keys of C, G and D major.

These intervals are in the same order as in the preceding Lessons, but are not divided by bars.

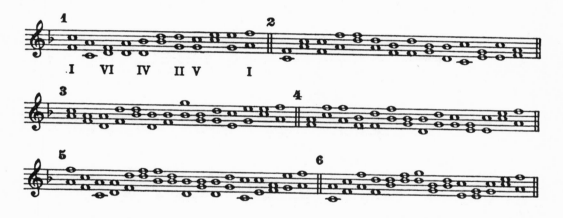

(3) *Exercises for Melodic Dictation and Sight-Singing,* containing the skip from 4-7 and ♪♪ and ♪♪ on the Up-beat in 6/8.

Practise:
   (a) Play the I, VI, IV, II, V and I chords in F major.
   (b) Read the melody mentally. Test.
   (c) Play the antecedent phrase twice. Sing from memory to *la.* Sing mentally the number-names; then use the letter-names. Sing aloud.
   (d) Practise the consequent phrase in the same way.
   (e) Play the entire melody. Sing from memory. In memorizing, keep a mental picture of the contour of the melody on the staff.
   (f) Stop for a moment and take breath at the end of each rhythmic figure, so as to feel the rhythmic grouping.

(g)   Sing again mentally without stopping. Be sure that the mind phrases or breathes properly.

(h)   Transpose to the keys of G and E major. Sing the letter- and number-names.

(i)   Have each melody dictated as outlined on page 19.

Section C.

(1)   *Absolute Intervals.*

There are major 6ths on the staff from c–a, d–b, f–d, g–e; in the major scale, from 1–6, 2–7, 4–2, 5–3; in the minor scale, from 2–7, 3–8, 4–2, 6–4. To sing a major 6th up, call the lower tone 5 and sing 3; to sing a major 6th down, call the upper tone 3 and sing 5.

    (a)   Play any tone on the piano, sing the tone calling it 5, then sing the tone a major 6th above, calling it 3.   Test.

    (b)   Play any tone on the piano, sing the tone calling it 3, then sing the tone a major 6th below, calling it 5.   Test.

    (c)   Repeat, singing the letter-names of the pitches.

(2)   *Rhythmic Study:*   The Up-beat in 6/8, ♫♫

    (a)   Study, using the arm movement to indicate the meter, and sing the rhythms to *la* on a major scale.

When the measure begins on the secondary pulse in 6/8 meter, avoid stressing the first group. Always feel the first figure as an inhalation of the breath, and the next, on the stressed pulse, as an exhalation. Feel the grouping as indicated by brackets in Ex. 1.

The value and rhythmic beauty of beginning on the secondary pulse in a compound meter is most apparent in the setting of words. With this understanding it is easily applied to instrumental music.

In setting words to music, the composer has to endeavor to parallel the forms of English with the forms in music, i.e., a simple sentence corresponds to a phrase in music, a compound sentence to a period in music. The meter, whether simple or compound, is decided by the number of long syllables in the complete thought of the text. If there are four long syllables the meter is duple or triple; if there are eight long syllables it is a compound, a four or six pulse meter.

A four pulse meter is a duple meter with each pulse divided into half

a six pulse meter, a duple meter with each pulse divided into triplets. The stress which is given to the third pulse of a four pulse meter and to the fourth pulse of a six pulse meter is known as a secondary accent. This is in reality the second or relaxed pulse of the duple meter and should not receive any more stress than that pulse. The tendency in playing and singing in compound meter is to give too much stress on the secondary pulse, thus changing the meter to a simple meter and making two phrases where one was intended.

Mendelssohn, in the "Elijah," in setting the following sentence begins on the third pulse in 4/4 meter:

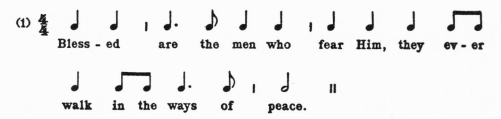

The sentence can also be read making *Blessed, men, they* and *way* the principal and stressed words. This changes the meaning of the sentence and would be set:

(2) 2/4 ♩ ♩. ♩. ♪ ♩. ♪ ♩ ♩
Bless - ed   are   the   men   who fear   Him,

♩ ♫♩ ♩ ♫ ♩. ♪ ♩
they   ev - er walk   in the   ways   of peace.

The tendency in singing this phrase as in 1 is to give too much stress on the word Blessed, and equal stress to each long syllable, making it sound like the

accented word as in 2, thus destroying the balance of the phrase, and making **two** phrases in duple meter. The only words which are stressed are the **first** words in each measure.

(3) *Practise the following Chord Successions.* In singing the first inversions, the arpeggio begins on the 3rd of the chord.

(a) Play the key-tone and sing mentally. Test for pitch.

(b) Sing the letter-, then the number-names.

(c) Sing to *la,* thinking the letter-, then the number-names.

(d) Have someone read aloud the symbols and sing the chords without reference to the written exercise. Keep a moderato tempo.

(e)   Sing the following chords to the rhythm of 2: I, VI₁, VI, IV₁, II₁, V, I; to the rhythm of 3: I, IV₁, IV, II₁, II, V, V₁, I; to the rhythm of 4: I, VI₁, VI, IV₁, IV, II₁, V, I.

(f)   Additional pitch drill. Sing the following exercises, first with the letter-names, then with the number-names:

   (1)   R of I, 3rd of I, R of IV, R of II, 3rd of II, 5th of II, 3rd of V, R of V, R of I.

   (2)   R of I, 5th of I, 3rd of VI, R of VI, 3rd of IV, 3rd of II, 3rd of V, 5th of V, 3rd of I, R of I.

   (3)   5th of I, 3rd of VI, 5th of IV, R of IV, 5th of II, R of II, 5th of V, 3rd of V, R of I.

   (4)   3rd of I, 5th of VI, R of IV, 5th of IV, R of II, 3rd of II, R of V, 5th of V, R of I.

Think the sound of the entire chord before singing the tone.

(4)   *Exercises for Sight-Singing:*

Lesson 6

A chord in the second inversion is used in three ways: in chord repetition

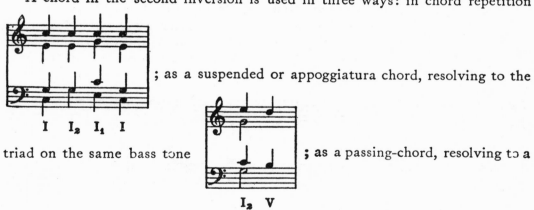

; as a suspended or appoggiatura chord, resolving to the

triad on the same bass tone ; as a passing-chord, resolving to a

triad or an inversion of a triad on the bass tone above or below:

In this Lesson the second inversions of the I and IV as appoggiatura chords
will be used.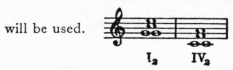

These chords occur generally on the accented pulse of the measure.

The second inversion of the I resolves to the V chord. As the 5th of the
chord is always doubled in second inversions, it sounds like and is often mistaken
for the V chord. It is generally used preceding the V chord at the authentic
cadence. It will be preceded by the I, I_1, IV, IV_1, VI, II or II_1.

The second inversion of the IV resolves to the I chord. Because of the
doubled 5th it sounds like the I chord. It may be preceded by the I, V, V_1, IV
or IV_1. This chord is sometimes used on the unaccented pulse as in Section B
(1) (5), and at the cadence, as in 8. This is known as a *Plagal Cadence*.

Section A.

(1) Construct parallel and contrasting periods in Bb major, using the I_2, IV_2
and all chords in fundamental position and first inversion as a basis for the melody.
Use 6/8 meter, beginning on the 4th pulse.

Study the rhythmic grouping of Lesson 5, Section C (2), page 47, and the
melodies in Section B (3), of this Lesson.

Section B.

(1) *Practise the following Chord Successions:*
  (a) Play each exercise, listening to the character of the chords and
       inversions.
  (b) Pause after each second inversion and think its resolution.
  (c) Read the exercise mentally. Test.
  (d) Have each exercise dictated. Work as outlined on page 4.

The I_2 and IV_2 are distinguished from each other by the chord of resolution. You hear the same effect of suspension for each, and determine that it
is the I_2 because it resolves to the V, or the IV_2 because it resolves to the I.

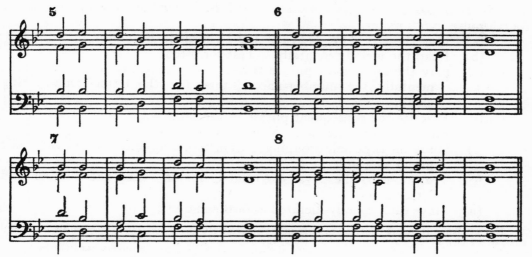

(2)   *Practise the following Intervals:*

(a)   Play the I, VI, IV, II, V and I chords in B♭ major.   Think the sound of the intervals.   Test.

(b)   Play the intervals, determining of what chord they are a part and how they sound in relation to the root of that chord and to the key-centre.

NOTE.   Beginning with this Lesson, the **intervals** do not occur in any fixed order.   They always follow, however, the correct harmonic sequence.   Intervals in the V chord will be followed by intervals in the I chord; in the II chord, by intervals in the V chord, etc.

(c)   Sing both tones of the intervals.

(d)   Transpose the intervals to the keys of C, G, D and F major.

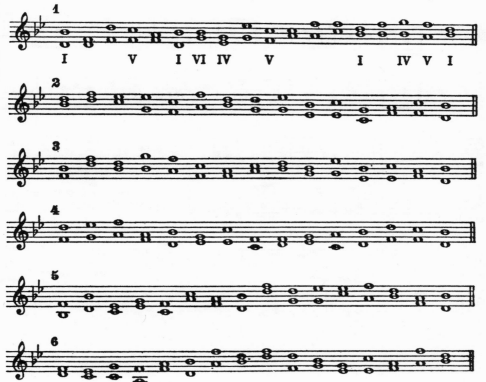

(3) *Exercises for Melodic Dictation and Sight-Singing,* beginning on the fourth pulse in 6/8 meter.

(a) Play the I, VI, IV, II, I₂, V and I chords in B♭ major.

(b) Read the melody mentally. Test for pitch.

(c) Play the antecedent phrase twice. Sing from memory to *la*. Sing mentally the number-names; then use the letter-names. Sing aloud.

(d) Practise the consequent phrase in the same way.

(e) Play the entire melody. Sing from memory.

(f) Study the rhythmic grouping. In memorizing consider each rhythmic group as a unit.

(g) Transpose to the keys of A and G major. Sing the number and letter names.

(h) Have each melody dictated as outlined on page 19.

NOTE. When there are consecutive skips in the same direction, do not think the separate tones, but analyze the chord. In Ex. 1, the third measure, the leaps down from the 3rd degree must be in the VI chord. In a melody like Ex. 6, third measure, do not try to remember the pitches: analyze as a scale from the 5th degree for six sixteenths ending on the next pulse.

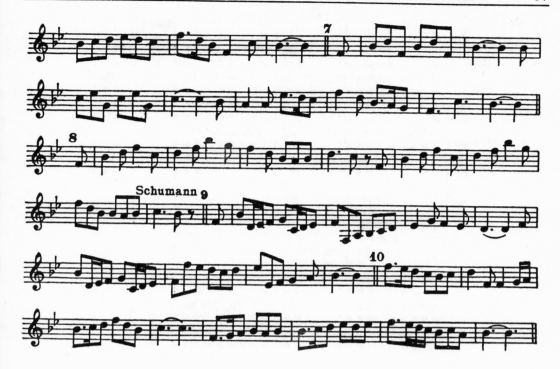

Section C.

(1) *Absolute Intervals.*

There are minor 6ths on the staff from e–c, a–f, b–g; in the major scale, 3–8, 6–4, 7–5; in the minor scale from 1–6, 5–3, 7–5. To sing a minor 6th up, call the lower tone 3 and sing 8; to sing a minor 6th down, call the upper tone 8 and sing 3.

(a) Play any tone on the piano; sing the tone, calling it 3; then sing the tone a minor 6th above, calling it 8. Test.

(b) Play any tone on the piano; sing the tone, calling it 8; then sing the tone a minor 6th below, calling it 3. Test.

(c) Repeat, singing the letter-names of the pitches.

(2) *Rhythmic Study:* 𝅘𝅥. 𝅘𝅥𝅯𝅘𝅥𝅯 and the Up-beat 𝅘𝅥𝅯, in 4/4 meter.

(a) Study, using the arm movement to indicate the meter, and sing to *la* on a major scale

In singing the figure 𝅘𝅥. 𝅘𝅥𝅯𝅘𝅥𝅯, which is the combination of a 𝅘𝅥 tied to 𝅘𝅥𝅯𝅘𝅥𝅯, 𝅘𝅥 𝅘𝅥𝅯𝅘𝅥𝅯, give a slight pressure on the dot so that the second pulse is perceptible to the listener. 𝅘𝅥 𝅘𝅥𝅯𝅘𝅥𝅯

NOTE. The Rhythmic Exercises following are all four measures long, as in the preceding Lessons, and are arranged in two braces on account of the number of notes in each exercise.

(3) *Practise the following Chord Successions.* In singing the second inversions of chords, the arpeggio will begin on the 5th of the chord.

 (a) Play the key-tone and sing mentally. Test for pitch.

 (b) Sing the letter-, then the number-names.

 (c) Sing to *la* thinking the number-, then the letter-names.

 (d) Have the chord symbols read and sing the chords without reference to the written exercise.

NOTE. In reading be sure the eye takes in the arpeggio as a unit. This saves the labor of reading each note and allows the mind to concentrate upon the rhythmic difficulties.

(e) Sing the following chords to the rhythm of 1: I, IV, I$_2$, V, I; to the rhythm of 2: I, I$_1$, IV, II$_1$ I$_2$, V, V$_1$, I; to the rhythm of 3: I, IV$_2$, I, V$_2$, I$_1$, IV, II$_1$, I$_2$, V, I; to the rhythm of 4: I, IV$_2$, V$_1$, V$_2$, I$_1$, I, I$_2$, V, I.

(f) Sing the exercises for pitch drill on page 50 in the key of B♭.

(4) *Exercises for Sight-Singing:*

CHAPTER III

CHORDS OF THE SEVENTH AND NINTH

All *Seventh* and *Ninth-Chords* are *Dissonant,* because of the major and minor 7th and 9th, formed by adding one or two more thirds to the triad.

The most used seventh-chords are the V^7 and II^7. The IV^7, VI^7, I^7 and III^7 are also used, but the 7th of each of these chords sounds like a suspended tone and not as a legitimate part of the chord.

$$V^7 \quad II^7 \quad IV^7 \quad VI^7 \quad I^7 \quad III^7$$

The most commonly used ninth-chord is the V^9,

$$V^9$$

LESSON 7

The V^7 chord is a major discord on account of the major 3rd from the 5th to the 7th degrees of the scale and the minor seventh from the 5th to the 4th degrees of the scale:

$$V^7$$

The V^7 chord is used the same as the V chord. The 7th of the chord, the 4th degree of the scale, must always resolve downward. Its resolution may be delayed by progressing up to the 5th degree and then down to the 3rd, or down to the 2nd and then to the 3rd while the V chord is held. This is known as a

delayed resolution:

$$V^7 \qquad I$$

Section A.

(1) Construct parallel and contrasting periods in G major and g minor, using all triads and inversions and the V^7 chord as a basis. Use the rhythmic figure 𝅘𝅥𝅭 𝅘𝅥𝅮𝅘𝅥𝅮 in 4/4 meter.

Section B.

(1) *Practise the following Chord Successions:*
   (a) Play each exercise, listening to the character of the chords and inversions.
   (b) Pause after each V^7 and think its resolution.

(c)   In place of each V⁷ play the V chord, then the V⁷.   Note the difference in sound.

(d)   Read the exercise mentally.

(e)   Have each exercise dictated.   Work as outlined on page 4.

The V^7 is distinguished from the V on account of the dissonance.

NOTE. Have the exercise played slowly. During the first playing relax and listen to the chords so that the entire exercise makes an impression upon the mind. Do not try to analyze at the first playing. During the second playing write down the chord symbols. At first it may be necessary to have the exercise played a second time for the symbols; next have it played and write the numbers of the scale-steps of the soprano. Compare your version with the exercise and correct mistakes by playing the mistake and then the correct version until the difference is heard.

(2)   *Practise the following Intervals:*

There are four new intervals in the V⁷ chord: the minor 7th from the root to the 7th of the chord, from the 5th to the 4th degrees of the scale; the major 2nd from the 7th to the root of the chord, from the 4th to the 5th degrees of the scale; the augmented 4th from the 7th to the 3rd of the chord, from the 4th to the 7th degrees of the scale; the diminished 5th from the 3rd to the 7th of the chord, from the 7th to the 4th degrees of the scale.

- (a)   Play the I, IV, V⁷ and I chords in g minor.   Think the sound of the intervals.   Test.
- (b)   Play the intervals, determining of what chord they are a part and how they sound in relation to the root of the chord and to the key-centre.
- (c)   Sing both tones of the intervals.
- (d)   Transpose the intervals to the keys of f, d, g and c minor.

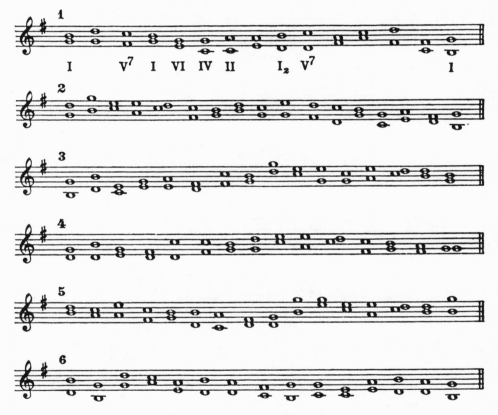

(3)   *Exercises for Melodic Dictation and Sight-Singing,* employing skips in the V⁷ chord and the rhythmic figure ♩. ♫ in 4/4 meter.

- (a)   Play the I, IV, V⁷ and I chords in g minor.
- (b)   Read the melody mentally.   Test.
- (c)   Play the antecedent phrase twice.   Sing from memory to *la.*   Sing mentally the number-names; then use the letter-names.   Sing aloud.
- (d)   Practise the consequent phrase in the same way.

(e)   Play the entire melody.   Sing from memory.

(f)   Transpose to the keys of a and f minor.   Sing the number- and letter-names.

(g)   Have each melody dictated as outlined on page 19.

NOTE.   In harmonizing a melody in 4-4, use a chord or inversion on each pulse.   In analyzing the rhythmic figure ♩. ♫ , note that the two sixteenths group themselves with the next pulse.   In analyzing, on account of the length of the ♩. there is danger of counting one, two and calling it a half-note, not waiting for the two sixteenths.   If ever in doubt about the rhythm, make an outline of the pulses, sing the tune, placing your pencil on a dot as the pulse recurs.   In this way the figure is easily analyzed.

Section C.

(1) *Absolute Intervals.*

There are minor 7ths on the staff from d–c, e–d, g–f, a–g, b–a; in the major scale, from 2–8, 3–2, 5–4, 6–5, 7–6; in the minor scale from 2–8, 4–3, 5–4; in all chords but the IV⁷ and I⁷. All of the 2nds on the staff are major except e–f, b–c; in the major scale, all but 3–4, 7–8; in the minor scale, all but 2–3, 5–6, 7–8; in all chords but the IV⁷ and I⁷. To sing a minor 7th up, call the lower tone 5 and sing 4; to sing a minor 7th down, call the upper tone 8 and sing 2. To sing a major 2nd up, call the lower tone 1 and sing 2; to sing a major 2nd down, call the upper tone 5 and sing to 4.

(a) Play any tone on the piano, and sing a minor 7th up, using first the number-names, then the letter-names.

(b)   Play any tone on the piano, and sing a minor 7th down, using first the number-names, then the letter-names.

(c)   Play any tone on the piano and sing a major 2nd up, using first the number-names, then the letter-names.

(d)   Play any tone on the piano and sing a major 2nd down, using first the number-names, then the letter-names.

(2)   *Rhythmic Study:* ♫ ₁ and ♪♫ ₁ on the Up-beat in 4/4 meter.

(a)   Study using the arm movement to indicate the meter, and sing to *la* on a major scale.   Always begin on the 8th degree of the scale and sing down.

(2)   *Practise the following Chord Successions.*   In singing the V⁷ chord, sing to the 7th of the chord and back; do not go to the octave:

(a)   Sing mentally.   Test for pitch.

(b)   Sing the letter-, then the number-names.

(c)   Sing to *la*, thinking the letter-, then the number-names.

(d)   Have the chord symbols read and sing the chords without reference to the written exercises.

(e) Sing the following chords to the rhythm of 1: I, V, V⁷, V⁷₃, I₁, IV, I₂, V⁷, I; to the rhythm of 2: I, VI, I₂, V⁷, VI, IV, I₂, V⁷, I; to the rhythm of 3: I, V²₂, V⁷₃, I₁, I₂, V⁷, V₁, I; to the rhythm of 4: I, IV₂, I, I₁, IV, IV₁, I₂, V⁷, I.

(f) Exercises for Pitch and Key Drill. Sing with number-, then letter-names, in the key of g minor. Think the sound of the entire chord before singing the tone.

   (1) R of I, 5th of I, R of V⁷, 3rd of V⁷, 5th of V⁷, 7th of V⁷, 3rd of I, R of IV, 5th of I, 3rd of V⁷, R of I.

   (2) R of I, 5th of V⁷, 3rd of I, R of IV, 5th of I, 3rd of IV, 5th of II, 3rd of V⁷, R of I.

   (3) 3rd of I, 7th of V⁷, 5th of V⁷, R of I, 3rd of VI, 5th of IV, 3rd of IV, R of V, 3rd of V⁷, R of I.

   (4) 5th of I, R of V⁷, 7th of V⁷, 3rd of V⁷, 3rd of I, R of I, R of IV, 3rd of I, 5th of I, 5th of V⁷, R of I.

(4) *Exercises for Sight-Singing:*

Brahms

Lesson 8

When the V^7 chord is inverted all four tones will resolve according to the melodic law. The V_1^7 will resolve to the I; 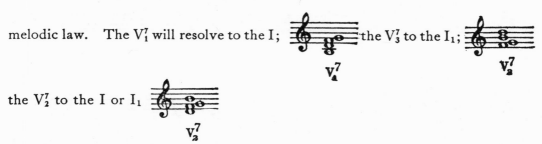 the V_3^7 to the I_1; the V_2^7 to the I or I_1

The root of the V^7 chord may be omitted, leaving the 7th, 2nd and 4th degrees of the scale. This is known as the $_0V^7$ (five-seven incomplete), and is the VII chord. All of the tones in this chord resolve melodically and like the upper voices of the V^7 chord. The $_0V^7$ is best used in the first inversion.

Section A.

(1) Construct parallel and contrasting periods in D major and d minor, using all triads and inversions and the V_1^7 and V_3^7 chords as a basis. Use the up-beats ♫ and ♪♫ in 4/4 meter.

Section B.

(1) *Practice the following Chord Successions*, which use the V_1^7 and V_3^7.

    (a) Play each exercise, listening to the character of the chords and inversions.

    (b) Pause after each V^7 inversion and think the chord of resolution.

    (c) Read each exercise mentally.

    (d) Have each exercise dictated.   Work as outlined on page 4.

On hearing the V^7 inversions, you will determine first that it is a V^7 chord; that it is inverted, because of the diatonic progression of the voices; that it is a V_1^7 because the I fundamental follows, or a V_3^7 because the I_1 follows.   The V_1^7 affects the ear as contracting when it resolves; the V_3^7 as expanding.

(2)   *Practise the following Intervals:*

The minor 7th and major 2nd, augmented 4th and diminished 5th in the V^7 chord are the same in minor as in major.   There is also an augmented 4th and diminished 5th in the II chord in minor, caused by the lowering of the 6th degree. The augmented 4th is from the 5th to the root of the chord, the 6th to the 2nd degrees of the scale, and the diminished 5th from the root to the 5th of the chord, the 2nd to the 6th degrees of the scale.

   (a)   Play the I, IV, II, V^7 and I chords in d minor.   Think the sound of the intervals.   Test.
   (b)   Play the intervals, determining of what chord they are a part and how they sound in relation to the root of the chord and to the key-centre.
   (c)   Sing the lower tones of the intervals, think the upper tones. Sing the upper tones and think the lower.
   (d)   Transpose the intervals to the keys of g, f and c minor.

   NOTE.   The augmented 4th in the II chord generally resolves to the minor 6th in the I chord; the diminished 5th to the major 2nd in the V^7 chord.

(3)   *Exercises for Melodic Dictation and Sight-Singing:*

Skips in the V^7 chord and the Up-beat ♫ and ♪♫ in 4/4 meter.

Observe carefully the rhythmic grouping with the up-beat ♫ or ♪♫

No. 1

No. 6

(a) Play the I, V⁷ and I chords in d minor and read the melody mentally, using the arm movement to beat the meter.
(b) Play the antecedent phrase twice. Sing the melody to *la*. Sing mentally the number-names, then the letter-names. Sing aloud.
(c) Practise the consequent phrase in the same way.
(d) Play the entire melody. Sing from memory.
(e) Transpose to the keys of e and c minor. Sing the number- and letter-names.
(f) Have each melody dictated as outlined on page 19.

Section C.

(1)   *Rhythmic Study:* ♩.. ♪ and ♩♪♪♪ (3) in 4/4 meter.

    (a)   Study using the arm movement to indicate the meter, and sing to *la* on a major scale.

NOTE. Do not confuse the rhythmic figure ♩. ♪, which is ♩ ♫, with ♩.. ♪, which is ♩ ♫.. . While holding the ♩. , mentally divide the pulse into halves, and the sixteenth notes will give no trouble.

(2)   *Practise the following Chord Successions.* Watch carefully that the augmented 4th in the V⁷ chord is in tune:

    (a)   Sing mentally. Test.

    (b)   Sing the letter-, then the number-names.

    (c)   Sing to *la*, thinking the letter-, then the number-names.

    (d)   Have the chord symbols read and sing the chords without reference to the written exercise.

(e) Sing the following chords to the rhythm of 1: I, IV, V_3^7, I_1, $_0V_1^7$, I, VI, V^7, V_1^7, I; to the rhythm of 2: I, VI, I_2, V^7, VI, VI_1, $_0V_1^7$, $_0V^7$, I; to the rhythm of 3: I, $_0V_1^7$, I, V_3^7, I_1, V_2^7, V_1^7, I, $_0V^7$, I; to the rhythm of 4: I, $_0V^7$, I, $_0V_1^7$, I_1, IV, V_3^7, I_1, $_0V_1^7$, I.

(f) Exercises for pitch and key drill. Sing with number-, then with letter-names in the key of d minor.

    (1) R of I, 3rd of I, R of IV, 5th of $_0V^7$, 3rd of $_0V^7$, R of $_0V^7$, R of I.

    (2) 3rd of I, R of IV, 7th of V^7, 3rd of V^7, R of V^7, R of I, 5th of I, R of VI, 3rd of IV, R of V, R of $_0V^7$, R of I.

    (3) 5th of I, 3rd of I, R of IV, 3rd of $_0V^7$, R of $_0V^7$, R of I, R of VI, 3rd of IV, R of IV, 7th of V^7, 5th of $_0V^7$, 3rd of $_0V^7$, R of I.

    (4) R of I, 3rd of $_0V^7$, 5th of $_0V^7$, 3rd of I, 3rd of IV, R of V^7, 3rd of V^7, R of $_0V^7$, 3rd of $_0V^7$, R of I.

(3) *Exercises for Sight-Singing:*

LESSON 9

The *Double Period Form* is two periods, or four phrases, having three semi-cadences, or imperfect authentic cadences, and one perfect authentic cadence.

The cadence at the end of the first phrase is generally an imperfect authentic cadence, the melody ending on 3 or 5; the cadence at the end of the second phrase is a semicadence, the melody ending on 5, 7 or 2; the cadence at the end of the third phrase is best made on some tone of the IV chord; the last cadence is a perfect authentic cadence.

The double period is in *parallel construction* when the first and third, and the second and fourth phrases are alike, except for the cadences and slight modifications.

The double period is in *contrasting construction* when the phrases are different.

The V^9 (five-nine) chord is made by adding another third to the V^7 chord.

V^9

In major this chord is not inverted, and the 9th of the chord is best in the soprano. In minor it may be inverted, but the 9th must be nine tones from the root.

The $_0V^9$ (five-nine incomplete) chord, or the VII^7 chord, is the V^9 with the

root omitted. This chord is more used than the V^9.

$_0V^9$

In major the $_0V^9$ may be inverted and all inversions but the third are used. This is not available, because the 7th of the chord must be above the root or it sounds like a VI chord with the 7th, 2nd and 4th degrees of the scale suspended. In minor the $_0V^9$ chord is a *diminished seventh-chord* (a chord the tones of which are a minor 3rd apart), and all inversions are used. All the voices of this chord resolve melodically.

Section A.

(1) Construct parallel double periods in F major and f minor, taking the melodies in Section B (3) as models and using all triads and inversions, the V^7

and V^9 chords as a basis. Use the rhythmic figures ♩.. ♪ and ♫ in 4/4 meter.

Section B.

(1) *Practise the following Chord Successions* which use all inversions of the V^7.

The V_2^7 resolves to the I or the I_1. When it resolves to the I_1 the 7th of the chord, the 4th degree of the scale, will go up so as to avoid doubling the 3rd of the I chord. This sounds well because of the parallel thirds between the bass and the

7th of the chord.

I V_2^7 I_1

(a) Play the entire exercise, listening to the character of the chords and inversions. At the first playing do not analyze. Allow the sound of the chords to make an impression upon the mind.

(b)   Pause after each V⁷ inversion and think the chord of resolution.
(c)   Read each exercise mentally.
(d)   Have each exercise dictated.   Work as outlined on page 4.
(e)   After working these exercises in F major, repeat in f minor.

The V_2^7 will be recognized as going down to the I chord, or up to the I_1.

(2)   *Practise the following Intervals:*

In the V⁹ chord there is a major 9th from the root to the 9th of the chord, the 5th to the upper 6th degree of the scale.   In minor this is a minor 9th.

In the $_0V^9$ chord there is a minor 7th from the root to the 7th of the chord, the 7th to the 6th degree of the scale. In minor this is a diminished 7th.

- (a) Play the I, IV, V^9, V^9_6, V^7_1 and I chords in F major. Think the sound of the intervals. Test. Play several times any interval you cannot hear mentally, then go back and read from the beginning. Repeat until you know the interval.
- (b) Play the intervals, determining how they sound in relation to the root of the chord and to the key-centre.
- (c) Sing the lower tones of the intervals, think the upper tones.
  Sing the upper tones and think the lower.
- (d) Transpose the intervals to the keys of B♭, D, G and C major.

I IV v⁷ v⁹ v⁷ I VI IV II v⁷ v⁹ v⁷ I

(3) *Exercises for Melodic Dictation and Sight-Singing:*

Double Periods in form. Skips in the V^9 chord and the rhythms

and in 2/4, 3/4, 4/4 meter.

- (a) Play the I, IV, II, V^9, V^7 and I chords in F major. Read the entire melody mentally. Test for pitch.
- (b) Play the entire melody, noticing the effect of the semicadences in continuing the thought for sixteen measures.

(c) Play the first antecedent phrase twice. Sing from memory to *la*. Sing the letter- and number-names, first mentally, then aloud.

(d) Practise the first consequent phrase in the same way.

(e) Play the first period and sing from memory.

(f) Practise the second antecedent and consequent phrases in the same way.

(g) Play the entire double period and sing from memory. This is easily accomplished if the construction of the melody is clearly understood.

(h) Transpose to the keys of E and G major.

(i) Sing melodies 2, 3, 5 and 6 in f minor.

(j) Have each melody dictated.

  (1) Play the entire double period. The pupil determines the meter by the number of pulses in a phrase, and the form by the number of cadences in the melody.

  (2) Play the first antecedent phrase twice. The pupil listens and memorizes the phrase.

  (3) The pupil analyzes and writes the phrase upon the staff.

  (4) Play again for correction.

  (5) Dictate the other phrases in the same way.

  (6) The pupil marks the form, figures, repetitions and sequences, and harmonization.

The figure ♩♫♬ is really a "turn," and will be recognized as such.

The figure ♩.. ♪ must be carefully contrasted with ♩. ♪ in dictating.

Section C.

(1) *Absolute Intervals.*

There is an augmented 4th on the staff from f–b; in the major scale from 4–7, 1–#4, b6–2, 6–#2, 3–#6; in the minor scale from 4–7, 6–2, 1–#4; in the V⁷, II⁷##, IIb⁷, ₀Vb⁹, and VI⁷## chords. There is a diminished 5th on the staff from b–f; in the major scale from 7–4, #4–1, 2–b6, #2–6, #6–3; in the minor scale from 7–4, 2–6, #4–8. To sing an augmented 4th up, call the lower tone 4 and sing 7; to sing an augmented 4th down, call the upper tone 7 and sing 4. To sing a diminished 5th up, call the lower tone 7 and sing 4; to sing a diminished 5th down, call the upper tone 4 and sing 7.

(a) Sing an augmented 4th up and a diminished 5th down from the following tones, using first the number-names, then the letter-names of the pitches:

(b) Repeat, singing the augmented 4th and its resolution, the minor 6th. Determine the key of which each interval is a part.

(c) Sing a diminished 5th up and an augmented 4th down from the following tones, using first the number-names, then the letter-names:

(d) Repeat, singing the diminished 5th and its resolution, the major 3rd. Determine of what key each is a part.

(2) *Rhythmic Study:*  in 4/4 meter.

(a) Study, using the arm movement to indicate the meter, and sing to *la* on a major scale. These exercises are to be practised very slowly, subdividing each pulse. The arm movement for sub-

divided pulses in 4/4 meter is 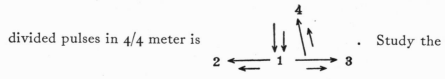 . Study the

rhythms mentally before attempting to sing them.

Repeat until the eyes can quickly grasp the beaming and group on each pulse. At first count *one and, two and, three and,* etc.; later only *one, two, three, four,* and make the subdivision mental.

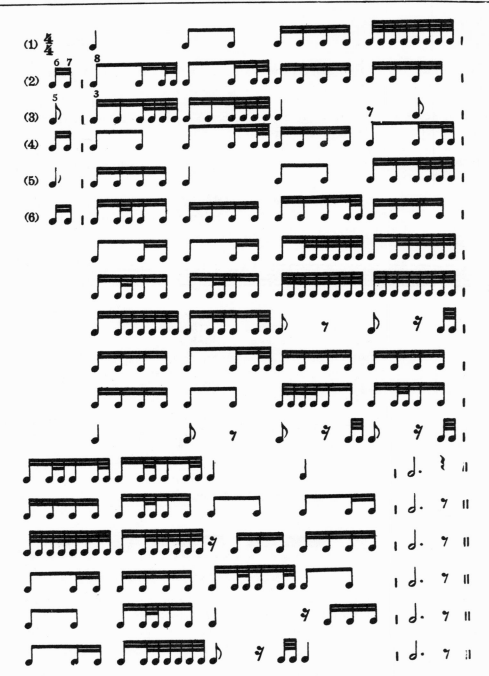

(3) *Practise the following Chord Successions.* Watch carefully that in the inversions of the V^9 and $_0V^9$ in minor the augmented 2nd, from the 6th to the 7th degree of the scale, is in tune.

    (a)   Sing mentally. Test.

    (b)   Sing the number-, then the letter-names.

    (c)   Sing to *la*, thinking the number-, then the letter-names.

    (d)   Have the chord symbols read and sing the chords without reference
          to the written exercise.

(e) Sing the following chords in the key of F major to the rhythm of 1: I, V_1^7, V_2^7, I_1, IV, II, V_1^7, $_0V^9$, I; to the rhythm of 2: I, V^9, $_0V^9$, $_0V_1^9$, I, I_1, IV, II_1, $_0V_2^9$, I_1, V_2^7, $_0V_1^9$, I.

Sing the following in the key of f minor to the rhythm of 3: I, VI, IV_1, V^7, V_1^7, I, $_0V^9$, $_0V_1^9$, I_1, V_2^7, I; to the rhythm of 4: I, I_1, $_0V_1^9$, $_0V^9$, I, IV, V, V^9, $_0V^9$, V_1^7, I.

NOTE Omit the 5th of the V^9 chord.

(f) Exercises for pitch and key drill in F major and f minor. Sing the number-, then the letter-names. Think the sound of the chord before singing the tone.

    (1) R of I, 5th of I, R of IV, 7th of V^7, 3rd of I, 5th of V, 7th of V^7, 9th of V^9, R of V, 3rd of V, R of I.

    (2) 3rd of I, 5th of VI, R of II, 9th of V^9, R of $_0V^9$, 3rd of V^7, R of I, 5th of IV, R of $_0V^9$, 7th of $_0V^9$, 5th of I.

(4) *Exercises for Sight-Singing:*

Wüllner

LESSON 10

The II[7] chord is formed by adding a third to the II triad. It is a minor discord because of the minor 3rd from the root to the 3rd of the chord, the 2nd to the 4th degrees of the scale, and the minor 7th from the root to the 7th of the chord, the 2nd to the 8th degree of the scale:

When the 8th degree of the scale is the 7th of a chord, it becomes an active tone and resolves downward to the 7th degree, as all 7ths of chords contract.

The II[7] chord may follow any chord but the V, and is followed by the V[7] or the I_2.

Section A.

(1) Construct parallel double periods in E♭ major, using all triads and inversions, the V[7], V[9], ₀V[9] and II[7] chords as a basis. Use the rhythmic figures

and

in 4/4 meter.

In writing melodies with thirty-second-notes it is difficult to slow down the mind. Think the subdivisions (the "*ands*") for each pulse. Study the rhythms in Section C of the preceding Lesson, page 90, and the melodies in Section B (3) of this Lesson.

Section B.

(1) *Practise the following Chord Successions:*
   (a) Play the entire exercise, listening to the character of the chords.
   (b) Pause after each II[7] and V[7] and think their resolutions.
   (c) Read each exercise mentally.
   (d) Have each exercise dictated.

The II[7] will be heard as a minor discord and will be distinguished from the V[7] because of its minor quality. The dissonance is harsher in quality because of the perfect 5th from the 3rd to the 7th of the chord.

(2) *Practise the following Intervals:*

The minor 7th in the II[7] chord, from the 2nd to the 8th degree of the scale, will resolve to some interval in the V[7] chord and will be distinguished by its resolution and context.

    (a)   Play the I, IV, II[7], V[7] and I chords in Eb major. Think the sound of the intervals.

(b) Play the intervals, determining how they sound in relation to the
root of the chord and to the key-centre. Note the difference in
relation to the key-centre of the three minor 7ths.

(c) Sing the intervals. Test for pitch.

(d) Transpose the intervals to the keys of B♭, F, G, D and C major.

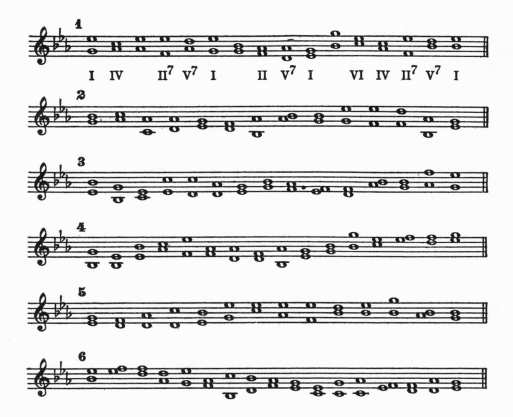

(3) *Exercises for Melodic Dictation and Sight-Singing:*

Double periods in form. Skips in the II[7] chord and thirty-second-notes in
duple and triple meter.

(a) Play the I, IV, II[7], V[7] and I chords in E♭ and read the entire melody
mentally, beating the meter. Subdivide the pulse on account of
the slow tempo and the number of notes to a pulse.

(b) Play the entire melody, studying the effect of the cadences.

(c) Play the first antecedent phrase twice. Sing from memory to
la. Sing the letter- and number-names, first mentally, then aloud.

(d) Practise the first consequent phrase in the same way.

(e) Play the first period and sing from memory.

(f) Practise the second period in the same way.

(g) Play the entire double period and sing from memory.

(h) Transpose to the keys of F and D major.

(i) Have each melody dictated as outlined on page 87.

Section C.

(1) *Rhythmic Study:* 𝅘𝅥𝅭 𝅘𝅥𝅮𝅘𝅥𝅮 and 𝅘𝅥𝅭 𝅘𝅥𝅮 in 4/4 meter.

(a) Study using the arm movement to indicate the meter and sing to *la* on a major scale.

(2) *Practise the following Chord Successions.* Be careful that the 7th of the II⁷ chord is in tune.

- (a) Sing mentally. Test.
- (b) Sing the number-, then the letter-names.
- (c) Sing to *la*, thinking the number-, then the letter-names.
- (d) Have the chord-symbols read and sing the chords without reference to the written exercise.

(e) Sing the following chords in the key of E♭ to the rhythm of 1: I, I$_1$, IV, II$_1$, I$_2$, V$_3^7$, I$_1$, II^7, V^7, I; to the rhythm of 2: I, VI, IV$_1$, V^7, V$_1^7$, I, II^7, V$_2^7$, I; to the rhythm of 3: I, IV, I$_2$, V$_3^7$, I$_1$, IV, II^7, I$_2$, V^7, I; to the rhythm of 4: I, II^7, V$_2^7$, I, V$_1^9$, V$_3^7$, I$_1$, II^7, V^7, I.

(f) Exercises for pitch and key drill. Sing the number-, then the letter-names.

    (1) R of I, 5th of I, R of IV, 3rd of II^7, R of II^7, 7th of II^7, 3rd of V, R of V, 5th of V, R of I.

    (2) R of I, 3rd of IV, R of II^7, 7th of II^7, 5th of II^7, 9th of V^9, 7th of V^7, 3rd of V^7, 5th of V^7, R of I.

    (3) 5th of I, 3rd of IV, 5th of II, 9th of V^9, R of V, 3rd of I, 3rd of II^7, 7th of II^7, R of II^7, 5th of II, R of I.

    (4) 3rd of I, 5th of VI, 3rd of VI, 7th of II^7 3rd of V, 7th of V^7, 9th of V^9, 5th of I, 3rd of II^7, R of II^7, 5th of V, R of I.

For review, these chords should be sung in all the keys of the preceding lessons.

(3) *Exercises for Sight-Singing:*

Beethoven

Lesson II

The II[7] chord is used in all inversions.   The II$_1^7$ may resolve to the V, V[7], V$_3^7$

or I$_2$; the II$_2^7$ to the V, or I$_2$; the II$_3^7$ to the V$_1^7$ or $_0$V[9].

II$_1^7$ II$_2^7$ II$_3^7$

Section A.

(1)   Construct parallel double periods in A major, using all triads and inversions, the V[7], V[9] and II[7] chords as a basis. Use the rhythmic figures

♪♪♪ , ♩.♪♪ and ♩..♪ in duple and triple meters.

Section B.

(1)   *Practise the following Chord Successions:*
These exercises are in period form, so there will be a pause in the fourth measure on the V chord for the semicadence.

(a)   Play the entire exercise, listening to the character of the chords and inversions and the effect of the semicadence.

   (b)   Pause after each II^7, II$_1^7$ and V^7 inversion and think the chord of resolution.

   (c)   Read the exercise mentally.

   (d)   Have each exercise dictated.

The II$_1^7$ will be distinguished from the II^7 by the diatonic progression of the voices.

  (2) *Practise the following Intervals:*

    (a)   Play the I, IV, II$_1^7$, V^7 and I chords in A major. Think the sound of the intervals.

(b)   Play the intervals, determining how they sound in relation to the
      root of the chord and to the key-centre.
(c)   Sing the intervals.   Test.
(d)   Transpose the intervals to the keys of E♭, B♭, F, G, D and C.

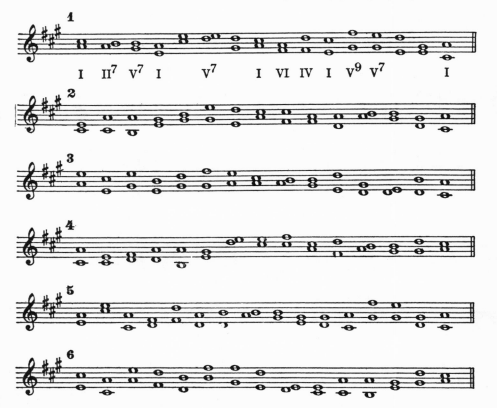

(3)   *Exercises for Melodic Dictation and Sight-Singing:*
Double periods in form.   Skips in the II[7] chord.   The rhythmic figures

and ... in duple and triple meter.

(a)   Play the I, IV, II[7], V[7] and I chords in A major.   Read the entire
      melody mentally, using the arm movement to indicate the meter.
(b)   Play the entire melody, studying the effect of the cadences.
(c)   Play the first antecedent phrase twice and sing from memory to *la.*
      Sing the number- and letter-names, first mentally, then aloud.
(d)   Practise the first consequent phrase in the same way.
(e)   Play the entire first period and sing from memory.
(f)   Study the second period in the same way.
(g)   Play the entire double period and sing from memory.
(h)   Transpose to the keys of G and B♭ major.
(i)   Have the melodies dictated as outlined on page 87.

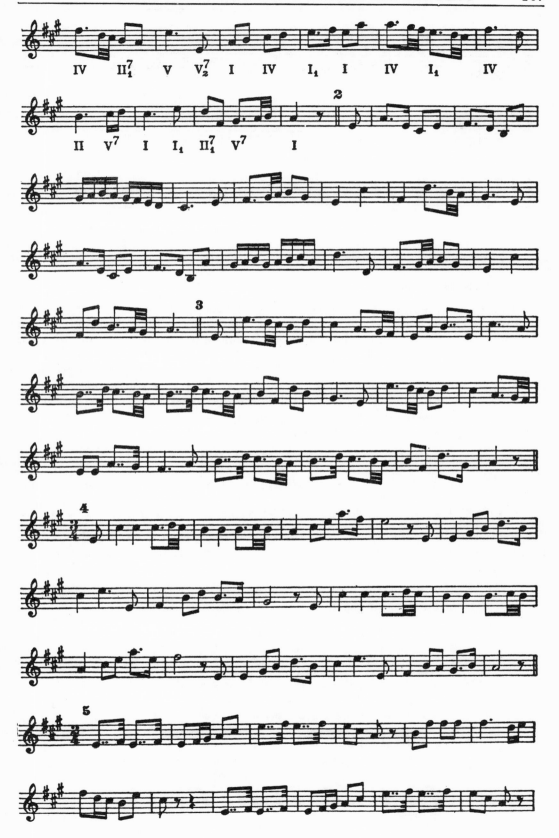

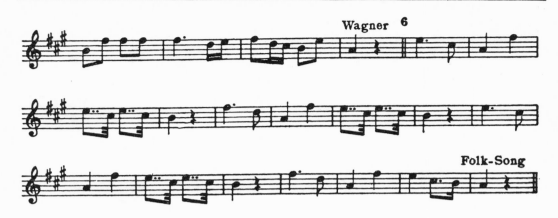

Section C.

(1)   *Rhythmic Study.*   Irregular Rhythms in 2/4 and 3/4.

Rhythm is irregular when the shorter notes occupy the accented or stressed portions of the measure.   The metric stress is still on the first pulse, but as the rhythmic motion stops on the longer note, that note is brought into prominence and acquires an accent.   This is known as a *Rhythmic Accent.*   Care should be taken not to stress this longer note, as it has stress on account of its length, and that stress combined with the rhythmic accent would give a *sforzando.*

In setting the following lines, Mr. Johnstone has used duple meter and these

rhythms: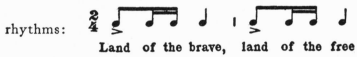

The natural inclination is to give all the stress upon the words "brave" and "free," thus giving the effect of beginning on the up-beat:

The stress should be on "land," and the rest of the measure a relaxation.   The words "brave" and "free" will receive proper stress on account of the length of the notes without any effort of the singer.

(a)   Study, using the arm movement to indicate the meter, and sing to
        la on a major scale.

(2)   *Practise the following Chord Successions:*

   (a)   Sing mentally.   It is most important that you think in tune.   If, at the end of the exercise, you are out of tune, go back and test at the end of each chord.   Do not play the exercise; only the key-tone.

   (b)   Sing the letter-, then the number-names.

   (c)   Sing to *la*, thinking the letter- and number-names.

   (d)   Sing from dictation.

(e) Sing the following chords in the key of A to the rhythm of 1: I, V, V_3^7, V_2^7, I_1, II^7, II_1^7, I_2, V^7, I; to the rhythm of 2: I, VI, II_1^7, I_2, V_3^7, I_1, II^7, II_3^7, V_1^7, V_2^7, I; to the rhythm of 3: I, IV_2, II_3^7, V_1^7, V_3^7, I_1, II_1^7, II_2^7, I_2, V^7, I; to the rhythm of 4: I, II_1^7, V_3^7, I_1, IV, IV_1, II_2^7, V^7, $_0V_2^9$, I_1, II^7, V^7, I.

(f) Sing the exercises for pitch and key drill of the preceding Lesson in the key of A major.

(3) *Exercises for Sight-Singing:*

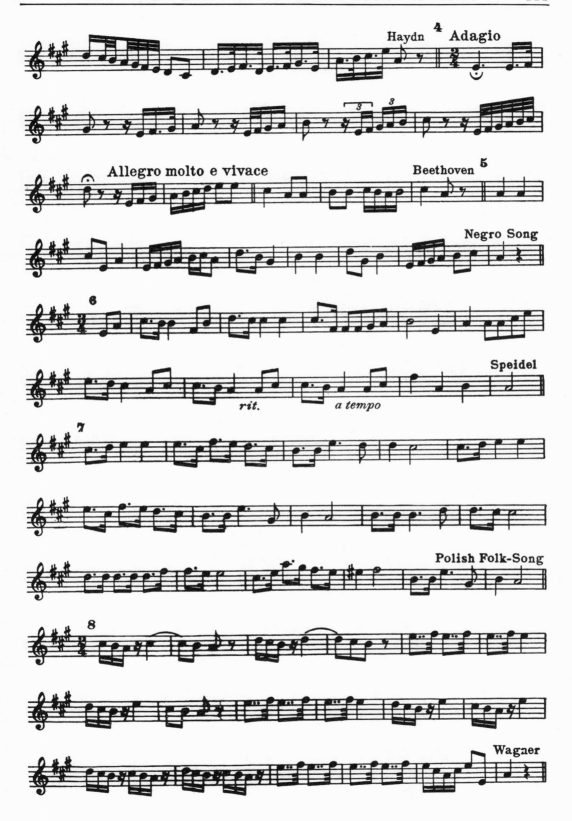

Folk-Dance

Folk-Dance

LESSON 12

The IV[7] chord is formed by adding a third to the IV triad. It is a major discord because of the major 3rd from the root to the 3rd of the chord, the 4th to the 6th degree of the scale, and the major 7th from the root to the 7th of the chord, the 4th to the 3rd degree of the scale.

$$IV^7$$

The 3rd degree of the scale, as the 7th of this chord, resolves downward to the 2nd degree.

The IV[7] chord may follow the I, VI or IV chords. It will be followed by the II[7]₁, V[7]₃ or I₂.

The IV[7] chord sounds like a II[7]₁ chord with a suspended 3rd degree of the scale.

Section A.

(1) Construct double periods in A♭ major, with the antecedent phrases alike and a new second consequent phrase. See melodies in Section B (3). Use all triads and inversions, the V[7], V[9], ₀V[9], II[7] and IV[7] chords as a basis. Use the irregular rhythms in 2/4 and 3/4 as given on pages 108 and 109.

Section B.

(1) *Practise the following Chord Successions:*

(a) Play the entire exercise, listening to the character of the chords and the effect of the semicadence.

(b) Pause after each II^7 and V^7 and think the chord of resolution.

(c) Read each exercise mentally.

(d) Have each exercise dictated.

The II_2^7 chord will be determined by its chord of resolution, the I_2 or V^7.

(2)   *Practise the following Intervals:*
The major 7th in the IV⁷ chord, from the 4th to the 3rd degree of the scale, will resolve to some interval in the V⁷ or II⁷ chord, or to the major 6th in the I₂ chord.

- (a)   Play the I, IV⁷, II⁷, V⁷ and I chords in the key of A♭ major.   Think the sound of the intervals.
- (b)   Play the intervals determining their sound in relation to the root of the chord and to the key-centre.
- (c)   Sing the intervals.   Test.
- (d)   Transpose the intervals to the key of E♭, B♭, F, G, D and C major.

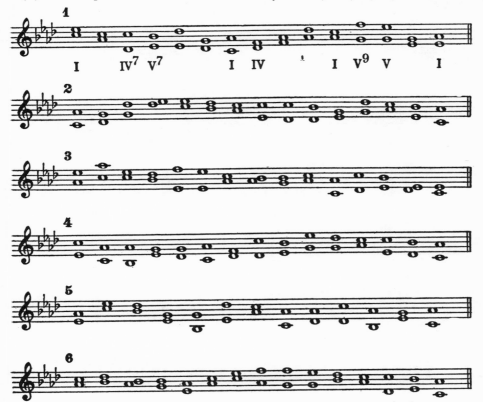

(3)   *Exercises for Melodic Dictation and Sight-Singing:*
Double periods with a new second consequent phrase.   Skips in the IV⁷ chord. Irregular rhythm in 2/4 and 3/4 meter.

- (a)   Play the I, VI, IV⁷, II⁷, V⁷ and I chords in A♭ major.   Read each melody mentally at a moderate tempo, using the arm movement to indicate the meter and thinking the rhythmic subdivisions.
- (b)   Play the entire melody, studying the effect of the cadences.
- (c)   Play the first antecedent phrase and sing from memory to *la.*   Sing the number-, then the letter-names.
- (d)   Practise the first consequent phrase in the same way.
- (e)   Play the entire first period and sing from memory.
- (f)   Study the second period in the same way.
- (g)   Play the entire double period and sing from memory.
- (h)   Transpose to the keys of G, F, and B♭ major.
- (i)   Have each melody dictated as outlined on page 87.

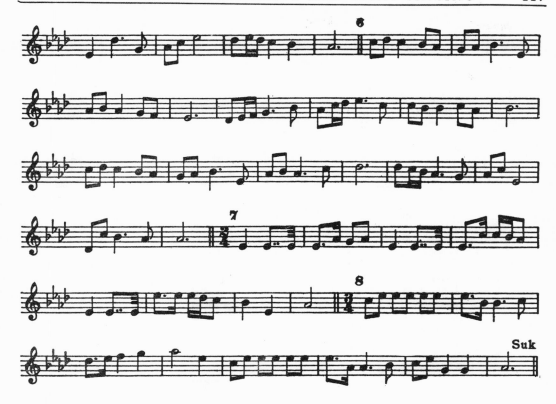

Suk

Section C.

(1) *Absolute Intervals.*

There are major 7ths on the staff from c–b, f–e; in the major scale from 1–7, 4–3; in the minor scale from 1–7, 3–2, 6–5; in the IV⁷ chord in major.   There are minor 2nds on the staff from e–f, b–c; in the major scale from 3–4, 7–8; in the minor scale from 2–3, 5–6, 7–8.   To sing a major 7th up call the lower tone 1 and sing 7; to sing a major 7th down call the upper tone 7 and sing 1.   To sing a minor 2nd up, call the lower tone 7, and sing 8; to sing a minor 2nd down, call the upper tone 8 and sing 7.

(a)   Play any tone on the piano and sing a major 7th up, using first the number-names, then the letter-names.

(b)   Play any tone on the piano and sing a major 7th down, using first the number-names, then the letter-names.

(c)   Play any tone on the piano and sing a minor 2nd up, using first the number-names, then the letter-names.

(d)   Play any tone on the piano and sing a minor 2nd down, using first the number-names, then the letter-names.

(2)   *Rhythmic Drill.*   Irregular rhythm in 4/4 meter.

(a)   Study, using the arm movement to indicate the meter, and sing to *la* on a major scale.

(2) *Practise the following Chord Successions:*
  (a) Sing each exercise mentally. Test.
  (b) Sing the number-, then the letter-names.
  (c) Sing to *la*, thinking the number- and letter-names.
  (d) Sing from dictation.

(e) Sing the following chords in the key of A♭ to the rhythm of 1: I, I$_2$, IV^7, V$_3^7$, I$_1$, IV, IV^7, I$_2$, V$_1^7$, I; to the rhythm of 2: I, VI, IV$_1^7$, V^7, V$_3^7$, I$_1$, IV, IV^7, II$_1^7$, V$_3^7$, I$_1$; to the rhythm of 3: I, IV$_2$, II$_3^7$, $_0$V^9, I, IV^7, II^7, V^7, V^9, I; to the rhythm of 4: I, IV, II^7, II$_1^7$, I$_2$, IV^7, V$_3^7$, V$_2^7$, I, IV$_2$, I.

(f) Exercises for pitch and key drill. Sing both the number- and letter-names.

   (1)   R of I, R of IV^7, 5th of IV^7, 7th of IV^7, 3rd of I$_2$, 5th of V, 7th of V^7, R of V^7, R of I, 7th of II^7, R of II^7, 3rd of V, 5th of V, R of I.

   (2)   3rd of I, 5th of VI, 7th of IV^7, 5th of V^7, R of I, 5th of I, R of IV^7, 7th of IV^7, R of II^7, 7th of II^7, 3rd of V, 7th of V^7, 3rd of V, R of I.

   (3)   5th of I, R of V, 9th of V^9, 7th of V^7, 3rd of I, R of II, 7th of IV^7, 7th of II^7, 9th of V^9, 7th of V^7, 5th of V^7, R of I.

(4) 3rd of I, 7th of II⁷, R of II⁷, 3rd of II⁷, 7th of V⁷, 3rd of V⁷, R of I, 3rd of IV⁷, 7th of IV⁷, 5th of IV⁷, 7th of II⁷, 3rd of V⁷, R of I.

(g) Transpose to other keys.

(3) *Exercises for Sight-Singing:*

LESSON 13

The VI[7] chord is formed by adding a third to the VI triad. It is a minor discord because of the minor 3rd from the root to the 3rd of the chord, the 6th to the 8th degree of the scale, and the minor 7th from the root to the 7th of the chord, the 6th to the 5th degree of the scale:

The 5th degree of the scale, as the 7th of this chord, resolves downward to the 4th degree.

The VI[7] chord may follow the I chord, and the VI chord.   It will be followed by any chord but the I.

The VI[7] chord sounds like the II[7] chord with the 3rd and 5th degrees of the scale suspended.

Section A.

(1) Construct double periods in F major, with a new second consequent phrase.   Use all triads, inversions, seventh- and ninth-chords as a basis for the melody.   Employ irregular rhythms 4/4 meter.

Section B.

(1) *Practise the following Chord Successions:*

In these exercises in triple meter the chord on the third pulse resolves to the chord on the first pulse; the chord on the second pulse is unrelated and allows foreign progression, the V to the IV or V to the II chord.

- (a) Play the entire exercise, listening to the character of the chords and inversions.
- (b) Pause after each II[7] and V[7] chord and think the chord of resolution. If you cannot hear mentally the chord of resolution, play it, then go back and try again.
- (c) Read the entire exercise mentally.
- (d) Have each exercise dictated.

The II$_3^7$ chord is recognized by its chord of resolution, the V$_1^7$, or by its diatonic introduction by the I chord.

(2) *Practise the following Intervals:*

The minor 7th in the VI⁷ chord will resolve to some interval in the IV⁷, II⁷ or V⁷ chord.

- (a) Play the I, VI⁷, IV⁷, II⁷, V⁷ and I chords in F major. Think the sound of the intervals.
- (b) Play the intervals, determining their sound in relation to the root of the chord and to the key-centre.
- (c) Sing the intervals. Test.
- (d) Transpose the intervals to the keys of E♭, B♭, G, D and C major.

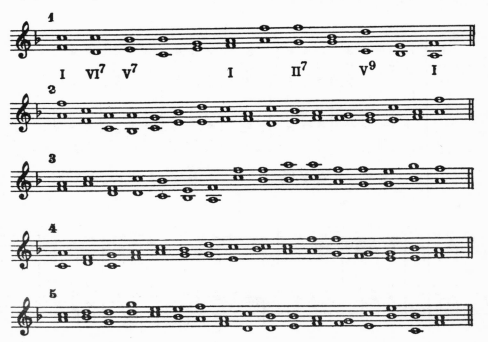

(3) *Exercises for Melodic Dictation and Sight-Singing:*
Double periods with new second consequent phrase.   Skips in the VI⁷ chord.
Irregular rhythm in 4/4 meters.

  (a) Play the I, VI⁷, II,⁷ V⁷ and I chords in the key of F major.   Read
       each melody mentally, using the arm movement to indicate the
       meter and thinking the rhythmic subdivisions.   Be careful not to
       overstress the rhythmic accents.
  (b) Play, studying the form.
  (c) Play the first antecedent phrase and sing from memory to *la*.   Sing
       the number-, then the letter-names.
  (d) Practise the first consequent phrase in the same way.
  (e) Play the entire first period and sing from memory.
  (f) Study the second period in the same way.
  (g) Transpose to the keys of E♭, D, G and A major.
  (h) Have each melody dictated as outlined on page 87.

Section C.

(1) *Rhythmic Drill.* Irregular rhythm in 3/4 meter.

    (a) Study, using the arm movement to indicate the meter, and sing to
        la on a major scale.

(2) *Practise the following Chord Successions:*
  (a) Sing each exercise mentally.   Test for pitch.
  (b) Sing the number-, then the letter-names.
  (c) Sing to *la*, thinking the number- and letter-names.
  (d) Sing from dictation.

(e) Sing the following chords in the key of F major to the rhythm of 1: I, $_0$V^9, I, VI^7, V$_1^7$, V^7, I, II$_3^7$, V$_1^7$, I; to the rhythm of 2: I, II$_3^7$, II$_2^7$, I$_2$, V$_3^7$, I$_1$, IV^7, I$_2$, II$_2^7$, V^7, I; to the rhythm of 3: I, II$_1^7$, I$_2$, $_0$V^9, I, VI^7, IV^7, V$_3^7$, I$_1$, II$_1^7$, I$_2$, V^7, I; to the rhythm of 4: I, IV, II$_1^7$, V$_3^7$, I$_1$, VI, VI^7, IV$_1^7$, V^7, I, II$_2^7$, I$_2$, V^7, I.

(f) Exercises for pitch and key drill. Sing both the number- and letter-names.

   (1) 5th of I, 7th of VI^7, 7th of V^7, 3rd of I, 7th of V^7, R of V, 3rd of V^7, 5th of V^7, R of I, 7th of IV^7, R of II^7, 5th of V, R of I.

   (2) 3rd of I, 7th of IV^7, 7th of II^7, 3rd of V, 7th of V^7, 3rd of I, 5th of VI^7, 7th of VI^7, 5th of I, 3rd of VI^7, 5th of IV^7, 7th of II^7 R of I.

   (3) R of I, 7th of II^7, 3rd of V^7, R of V^7, 5th of I, R of VI, 3rd of VI^7, R of IV, 7th of IV^7, R of II, 7th of II^7, 3rd of V^7, R of I.

   (4) 3rd of I, R of II^7, 3rd of II^7, 7th of V^7, 3rd of V^7, 3rd of I, 5th of I, 7th of VI^7, 7th of V^7, 3rd of I, 7th of IV^7, 3rd of I$_2$, 7th of V^7, 3rd of I.

(g) Transpose to other keys.

(3) *Exercises for Sight-Singing:*

Negro Song

CHAPTER IV

CHROMATICALLY ALTERED CHORDS

The pitch of the 1st, 2nd, 4th, 5th and 6th degrees of the major scale may be chromatically raised a half-tone, and the 2nd and 6th degrees chromatically lowered a half-tone, without disturbing the feeling of the tonality.

In using the scale-line these inflections must progress chromatically as chromatic passing-tones, never diatonically, or a modulation will occur: 3 4 #4 5 or

5 #4 ♮4 3, not 3 #4 5 or 5 #4 3 :

In minor, the 2nd and 5th degrees are not raised because of the lowered 3rd and 6th degrees. The 6th degree is raised in the melodic progression from the 6th to the 7th degree, and the 7th degree is lowered in the melodic progression from the 7th to the 6th degree.

In skips, single or consecutive, the altered tones must be part of a chord.

The #4, of the II⁷# or IV⁷# chord: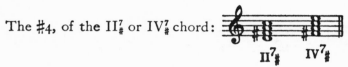

The #2, of the V#, V⁷#, V⁹# or the II⁷## in conjunction with the #4:

The #1, of the VI⁷#:

The #6, of the VI⁷## in conjunction with the #1:

The ♭6, of the II⁷♭, IV⁷♭ and V⁹♭:

The ♭2, of the V⁷₂♭ and ₀V⁹♭:

The ♭2 and ♭6 together in the II♭♭ and ₀V⁹♭♭:

[132]

The $\sharp4$ and $\flat6$ together in the $II^7_{2\sharp\flat}$ and $IV^7_{1\sharp\flat}$:

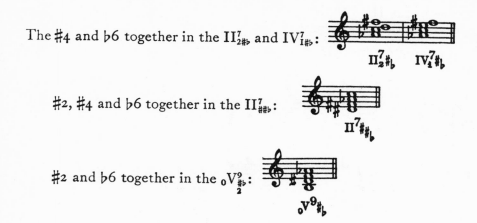

$\sharp2$, $\sharp4$ and $\flat6$ together in the $II^7_{\sharp\sharp\flat}$:

$\sharp2$ and $\flat6$ together in the $_0V^9_{\substack{\sharp\flat \\ 2}}$:

LESSON 14

The raised 4th degree is used as a chromatic passing-tone in progressing either from the 4th to the 5th degree, or from the 5th to the 4th degree:

Skips may be made from or to the raised 4th degree in the $II^7_\sharp$ chord. The scale-line using the natural 4th degree or skips in the V^7 or I chord should follow:

Section A.

(1) Construct double periods in C major, with a new second consequent phrase. Use all triads, inversions, seventh- and ninth-chords and the $II^7_\sharp$ chord as a basis for the melody. Employ irregular rhythms in 3/4 meter.

Section B.

(1) *Practise the following Chord Successions:*

The $_0V^9$ chord is a discord because of the minor 7th from the root to the seventh of the chord, the 7th to the 6th degree of the scale. The $_0V^9$ chord may be followed by the V^7_1, V or I chord.

    (a) Play the entire exercise, listening to the character of the chords and inversions.

    (b) Pause after each $_0V^9$, II^7 and V^7 and think the chord of resolution. Test.

    (c) Read the entire exercise mentally.

    (d) Have each exercise dictated.

The $_0V^9$ chord will often be confused with the II^7, as they have three tones in common, the difference being that the 7th degree of the scale is in the $_0V^9$

and the 1st degree in the II⁷. Play the II₃⁷ chord in place of the ₀V⁹, then the ₀V⁹, until you hear the difference.

(e) Repeat these exercises in c minor.

(2) *Practise the following Intervals:*

The following intervals, parts of the II♯⁷ chord, are used: The major 3rd from the root to the 3rd of the chord, the 2nd to the ♯4th degree of the scale; the minor 3rd from the 3rd to the 5th of the chord, the ♯4th to the 6th degree of the scale; the minor 6th from the 3rd to the 8th of the chord, the ♯4th to the

2nd degree of the scale; the major 6th from the 5th to the 3rd of the chord, from the 6th to the ♯4th degree of the scale.

- (a) Play the I, IV, II⁷, II⁷♯, V⁷ and I chords in C major. Think the sound of the intervals.
- (b) Play the intervals determining their sound in relation to the root of the chord and to the key-centre.
- (c) Sing the intervals. Test.
- (d) Transpose the intervals to c minor.

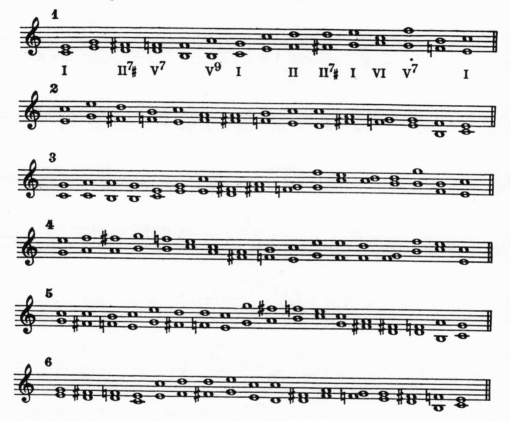

(3) *Exercises for Melodic Dictation and Sight-Singing:*

Double periods with new second consequent phrase. Skips in the II⁷♯ chord and the ♯4th degree used as a chromatic passing-tone. Irregular rhythm in 3/4 meter.

- (a) Play the I, IV, II⁷, II⁷♯, V⁷ and I chords in C major. Read each exercise mentally, using the arm movement to indicate the meter and thinking the rhythmic subdivisions.
- (b) Play, studying the effect of the chromatic tones.
- (c) Play the first antecedent phrase and sing from memory to *la*. Sing the number-, then the letter-names.
- (d) Practise the first consequent phrase in the same way.
- (e) Play the entire first period and sing from memory.
- (f) Study the second period in the same way.
- (g) Transpose to the keys of B, A, D and E major.
- (h) Have each melody dictated as outlined on page 87.

Section C.

  (1) *Rhythmic Drill.* Irregular rhythm in 6/8 meter.

     (a) Study, using the arm movement to indicate the meter, and sing to *la* on a major scale.

  (2) *Practise the following Chord Successions:*

     (a) Sing each exercise mentally. Test for pitch.

     (b) Sing the number-, then the letter-names.

     (c) Sing to *la*, thinking the number- and letter-names.

     (d) Sing from dictation.

(e) Sing the following chords in the key of C major to the rhythm of 1: I, IV, $II^7_{1\sharp}$, I_2, V^7_3, I_1, $II^7_\sharp$, V^7_2, I; to the rhythm of 2: I, II^7, II^7_3, $II^7_{3\sharp}$, $_0V^9$, I, $II^7_\sharp$, $II^7_{3\sharp}$, I_2, V^7, I; to the rhythm of 3: I, VI, IV_1, II^7_2, $II^7_{2\sharp}$, I_2, V^7_1, I, $II^7_\sharp$, $II^7_{3\sharp}$, V^7_1, I: to the rhythm of 4: I, IV^7, II^7_1, $II^7_{1\sharp}$, I_2, V^7_1, $_0V^9$, I, $II^7_\sharp$, $II^7_{1\sharp}$, V^7_3, V^7_2, I.

(f) Exercises for pitch and key drill. Sing both the number- and letter-names.

    (1)   R of I, 7th of II^7, 5th of $II^7_\sharp$, 3rd of $II^7_\sharp$, R of V^7, 7th of V^7, 3rd of I, R of $II^7_\sharp$, 3rd of $II^7_\sharp$, 7th of V^7, 3rd of V^7, R of I.

    (2)   3rd of I, R of IV, 3rd of $II^7_\sharp$, 7th of II^7, 3rd of V^7, 7th of V^7, 5th of I, 7th of VI^7, 3rd of $II^7_\sharp$, 5th of I_2, 5th of V^7, R of I.

    (3)   5th of I, 7th of IV^7, R of II^7, 5th of II^7, 3rd of II^7, 3rd of $II^7_\sharp$, 7th of V^7, 3rd of I, 7th of II^7, 3rd of $II^7_\sharp$, 3rd of II^7, 7th of V^7, 3rd of I, R of I.

    (4)   8th of I, 3rd of IV, 7th of IV^7, R of II^7, 7th of II^7, 3rd of II^7, 3rd of $II^7_\sharp$, 5th of I_1, 3rd of $II^7_\sharp$, 7th of V^7, 3rd of V^7, R of I.

(g) Transpose to other keys.

(3) *Exercises for Sight-Singing:*

LESSON 15

In a melody skips may be made from or to the raised 4th degree of the scale in the IV$_\sharp^7$ chord. The scale-line, using the natural 4th degree, or skips in the

II$_\sharp^7$, or I$_2$ V^7 chord, should follow:

Section A.

(1) Construct double periods in B♭ major, with a new second consequent phrase. Use all triads, inversions, seventh- and ninth-chords and the II$_\sharp^7$ and IV$_\sharp^7$ chords, as a basis for the melody. Employ irregular rhythms in 6/8 meter. See Section C of the preceding Lesson.

Section B.

(1) *Practise the following Chord Successions:*

  (a) Play the entire exercise, listening to the character of the chords and inversions.

  (b) Pause after each IV^7, II^7, V^7 and $_0V^9$ chord and think the chord of resolution.

  (c) Read the entire exercise mentally.

  (d) Have each exercise dictated.

The IV^7 chord sounds like a II^7 chord with the 3rd degree of the scale suspended.   Be sure the mind grasps the characteristic tone of difference between these chords.

(2) *Practise the following Intervals:*

In the IV$_\sharp^7$ chord there will be a minor 3rd from the root to the 3rd of the chord, the $\sharp$4th to the 6th degree of the scale; a diminished 5th from the root to the 5th of the chord, the $\sharp$4th to the 8th degree of the scale; a minor 7th from the root to the 7th of the chord, the $\sharp$4th to the 3rd degree of the scale.

(a) Play the I, IV^7, IV$_\sharp^7$, III$_{i\sharp}^7$, V^7 and I chords in B$\flat$ major. Think the sound of the intervals.

(b) Play the intervals determining their sound in relation to the root of the chord and the key-centre.

(c) Sing the intervals.

(d) Transpose the intervals to C major.

(3) *Exercises for Melodic Dictation and Sight-Singing:*

Double periods with a new second consequent phrase. Skips in the IV$_\sharp^7$ chord and the $\sharp$4th degree used as a passing-tone. Irregular rhythm in 6/8 meter.

(a) Play the I, IV, IV^7, IV$_\sharp^7$, I$_2$, V^7 and I chords in B$\flat$ major. Read each exercise mentally, using the arm the movement to indicate the meter and thinking the rhythmic subdivisions.

(b) Play, studying the effect of the chromatic tones.

(c) Play the first antecedent phrase and sing from memory to *la*. Sing the number-, then the letter-names.

(d) Practise the first consequent phrase in the same way.

(e) Play the entire first period and sing from memory.

(f) Study the second period in the same way.

(g) Transpose to the keys of C, D, A and G major.

(h) Have each melody dictated as outlined on page 87.

In all wide or consecutive skips, it is most important to remember the tone jumped from. In Ex. 1, measure 7, you hear chord-line from the 3rd degree down for three tones, then a skip back to the same tone. In that way you do not have to think of the large skip. Ex. 3, measure 6 and 7, if the pitch of "f" is remembered there is no difficulty in recognizing the "e♮". In Ex. 4, measure 3, remember "f," which will recur in 4; meas. 4, "d," which will recur in 5; meas. 5, "e♮" and "c," so as to get the "e♭" and "c" following.

Section C.

(1) *Rhythmic Drill:*

A tie and a dot have the same effect and are sung in the same manner, with a slight pressure on the tied note so as to preserve the pulse.

Rhythms which can be expressed by a dot are seldom expressed by ties, not

When holding a tied note, always think the subdivision which makes the next figure, i.e., if singing, think the triplet as the quarter is held; for the figure, think either two eighths or four sixteenths.

(a) Study, using the arm movement to indicate the meter, and sing the rhythms to *la* on a major scale.

(2)   *Practise the following Chord Successions:*
   (a)   Sing each exercise mentally.   Test.
   (b)   Sing to *la*, thinking first the number-, then the letter-names.
   (c)   Sing from dictation.

In singing these rhythms be sure that the mind takes in the rapid arpeggio as a unit.   While the tied note is being held, think the rhythm and arpeggio that is to be sung on the next pulse.

(d)   Sing the following chords in the key of B♭ major to the rhythm of 1: I, I₂, IV♭♯, V♭₃, V♭₂, I, II♭♯, II♭, V♭₁, I; to the rhythm of 2: I, VI♭, IV♭₁♯, I₂, IV♭♯, II♭₁♯, V♭₃, I₁, II♭₁, I₂, V♭, I; to the rhythm of 3: I, IV♭♯, V♭₃, I₁, II♭₂♯, I₂, II♭₁, II♭₁♯, I₂, V♭, I; to the rhythm of 4: I, II♭₃, II♭₃♯, ₀V♭, V♭₁, I, IV♭♯, II♭♯, I₂, V♭, I.

(e)   Transpose these exercises to other keys.

(f)   Sing the exercises for pitch and key drill of the preceding Lesson on page 138, in the key of B♭ major.

(3)   *Exercises for Sight-Singing:*

LESSON 16

In a melody the raised 2nd degree is used as a chromatic passing-tone between the 2nd and 3rd degrees and the 3rd and 2nd degrees. In progressing from the 3rd to the 2nd degree, the progression is often written 3, lowered 3 and 2. It will be found simpler and much less confusing in both harmonic and melodic relations in major to use the raised 2nd, never the lowered 3rd degree, as this is

the characteristic tone of the minor mode.

Skips may be made from or to the raised 2nd degree of the scale in the $II_{\sharp\sharp}^7$ chord. The scale-line, using the natural 2nd degree, or skips in the $II_\sharp^7$, II^7, V^7

or I chord, should follow.

Section A.

(1) Construct double periods in B major, with a new second consequent phrase. Use all triads, inversions, seventh- and ninth-chords, the $II_\sharp^7$, $IV_\sharp^7$, and $II_{\sharp\sharp}^7$, as a basis for the melody. Employ the rhythms given on page 145.

Section B.

(1) *Practise the following Chord Successions:*
   (a) Play the entire exercise, listening to the character of the chords and inversions.
   (b) Pause after each seventh-chord and think the chord of resolution.
   (c) Read the entire exercise mentally.
   (d) Have each exercise dictated.

(2) *Practise the following Intervals:*

In the $\text{II}^7_{\#\#}$ chord there will be a minor 3rd from the root to the 3rd of the chord, the #2nd to the #4th degree of the scale; a diminished 5th from the root to the 5th of the chord, the #2nd to the 6th degree of the scale; a diminished 7th from the root to the 7th of the chord, the #2nd to the 8th degree of the scale; a major 6th from the 3rd to the 8th of the chord, the #4th to the #2nd of the scale; an augmented 4th from the 5th to the 8th of the chord, the 6th to the #2nd degree of the scale; an augmented 2nd from the 7th to the 8th of the chord, the 8th to the #2nd degree of the scale.

(a) Play the I, IV^7, II^7, $\text{II}^7_{\#}$, $\text{II}^7_{\#\#}$, V^7 and I chords in B major. Think the sound of the intervals.

(b) Play the intervals determining their sound in relation to the root of the chord and to the key-centre.

(c) Sing the intervals.

(d) Transpose the intervals to C major.

(3) *Exercises for Melodic Dictation and Sight-Singing:*

Double periods with a new second consequent phrase. Skips in the $II^7_{\#\#}$ chord and the raised 2nd and 4th degrees used as passing-tones. The tie in 2/4, 3/4 and 4/4 meter.

- (a) Play the I, II⁷, $II^7_\#$, $II^7_{\#\#}$, I, V⁷ and I chords in B major. Read each exercise mentally. Test for pitch.
- (b) Play the entire melody, studying the effect of the cadences, the chromatic tones and the ties.
- (c) Take each section of the melody which has a chromatic inflection and sing it first without the altered tones, then as written.
- (d) Play the first antecedent phrase and sing from memory to *la*. Sing the number-, then the letter-names, mentally and aloud.
- (e) Practise the first consequent phrase in the same way.
- (f) Play the entire first period and sing from memory.
- (g) Study the second period in the same way.
- (h) Play the entire double period and sing from memory.
- (i) Transpose to the keys of C and B♭ major.
- (j) Have each melody dictated, as outlined on page 87.

Section C.

(1) *Rhythmic Drill:*

(a) Study, using the arm movement to indicate the meter, and sing the rhythms to *la* on a major scale.

(2) *Practise the following Chord Successions:*

(a) Sing each exercise mentally.   Test.
(b) Sing to *la*, thinking the number-, then the letter-names.
(c) Sing from dictation.

(d) Sing the following chords in the key of B major to the rhythm of 1: I, I₁, II⁷##, I₁, IV⁷, I₂, IV⁷#, II⁷#, V⁷₂, I; to the rhythm of 2: I, IV, V⁷₃, V⁷₂, I₁, II⁷##, II⁷₁##, II⁷₂##, I₂, V⁷, I; to the rhythm of 3: I, II⁷, II⁷##, I₁, IV⁷, II⁷##, V⁷₂, I, ₀V⁹, V⁷₁, I; to the rhythm of 4: I, IV₂, ₀V⁹, V⁷₁, I, II⁷₃, II⁷₃#, II⁷₃##, V⁷₁, V⁷₂, I.

(e) Exercises for pitch and key drill. Sing the letter- and number-names:
   (1) R of I, R of II⁷##, 3rd of II⁷##, 7th of V⁷, R of V⁷, 3rd of I, 3rd of IV, R of II⁷##, 3rd of I, 3rd of V, R of I.
   (2) 3rd of I, 3rd of II⁷#, R of II⁷#, R of II⁷##, 5th of II⁷##, 7th of V⁷, 5th of I, 7th of II⁷, 3rd of II⁷#, 7th of V⁷, 3rd of I.
   (3) 5th of I, 3rd of IV, 5th of IV, 7th of II⁷, R of II⁷##, 5th of II⁷##, 5th of I, R of IV, 3rd of V⁷, 5th of V⁷, R of I.
   (4) 3rd of I, 7th of II⁷##, R of II⁷##, 5th of II⁷##, 3rd of II⁷##, 3rd of I, 7th of V⁷, 5th of I, 3rd of V⁷, R of I.

(f) Sing this drill in the keys of B♭ and C major.

(3) *Exercises for Sight-Singing:*

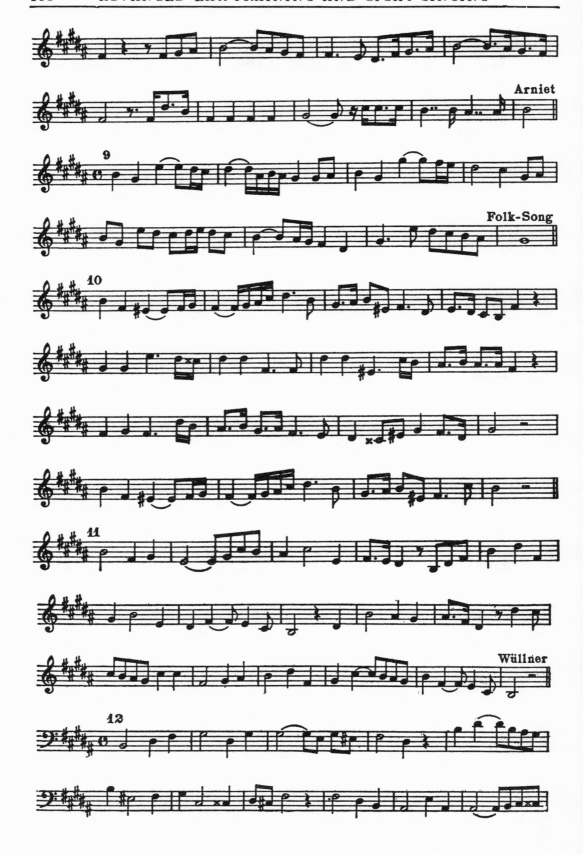

Arniet

Folk-Song

Wüllner

CHAPTER V

MODULATION AND EMBELLISHMENT

Modulation is the process of progressing from one key or mode to another. Modulations to the keys of the Dominant, Subdominant, the Relative Minor and the relative minor keys of the Dominant and Subdominant are most used; these are easily made because of the common tones and chords. Modulations to these keys are known as *Next-Related Modulations.*

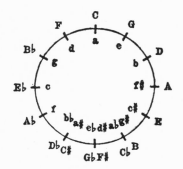

The next-related keys are those on either side of a key in the circle of keys, and have one accidental more or less in the signature.

In modulating, it is best to leave the key with the I chord on an accented pulse of the meter and to begin the new key with any chord but the I on an unaccented pulse of the meter.

Lesson 17

Modulation to the Dominant Key and back is by the V[7] or a common chord; e.g., the I chord of C is the IV chord of G; the V chord of C is the I chord of G; the VI chord of C is the II chord of G; the III chord of C is the VI chord of G.

| I of C | V of C | VI of C | III of C |
| IV of G | I of G | II of G | VI of G |

In Section B, Ex. 1, the first three chords establish the key of C major. The key of G begins with the IV chord, the second chord in the second measure. The first chord in the second measure is the I chord of C major, because it is the resolution of the preceding V chord. The next chord, though identical with the preceding chord, is the IV chord of G major, as it resolves into the I_2 chord over the bar. The same type of modulation is made from G back to C in the second phrase. In Ex. 2, the first chord in the consequent phrase is either the I of C or the V of G. In Ex. 3, the key of G begins with the V[9]: the I of C preceding is the IV of G. The consequent phrase begins with the V[9] of C. In Ex. 4, the second chord of the second measure is the I_1 of C, the resolution of the V_3^7 chord, and at the same time the IV_1 chord of G progressing over the bar into the I chord.

Section A.

(1) Construct parallel and contrasting periods in the key of C major, modulating to the key of the dominant and back. Employ the meters and rhythms given on page 154.

Work as in the preceding Lessons. Write the chord symbols and construct the melody from the chords. It is best not to modulate until there have been enough chords in the key to establish the tonality; in duple and quadruple meter at least three, and in triple meter at least four.

NOTE.—The IV or V chord progressing to the I chord establishes a key. When modulating in the period form the modulation to the key of the dominant is generally made in the antecedent phrase, so that the perfect cadence in the dominant key takes the place of the semicadence. See Ex. 1, Section B (1).

Section B.

(1) *Practise the following Chord Successions:*
  (a) Play the entire exercise slowly, listening to the character of the chords, if major or minor, active or rest, inverted or fundamental. Do not try to think the key.
  (b) Pause after the last chord in C and think the rest of the phrase. Pause after the last chord in G and think the rest of the phrase.
  (c) Sing the number-names of the soprano as you play.
  (d) Read the entire exercise mentally.
  (e) Have each exercise dictated.
    (1) As the entire exercise is played, relax and listen to the sound of the chords. Do not analyze.
    (2) As the chords are played a second time, write down the chord symbols as you hear them, regardless of key.
    (3) Write the numbers of the soprano. In Ex. 1 you will hear the first three numbers as 8, 7, 8; the next as 8; the next as 3, or possibly it will be uncertain; the next as 2, 1. The mind will reflect and hear 3, 2, 1. In that case the fourth pitch will have to be 4, as the unaccented pulse is always related to and progresses into the accented pulse. In the consequent phrase you will hear 3, 4, 3, then 5, then 3, 2, 1. The mind will reflect and make the fourth pitch 2, resolving up to 3 over the bar.
    (4) Next, write the absolute pitches of the soprano. In Ex. 1 you will have c, b, c as 8, 7, 8; then c as 4, b as 3, a as 2 and g as 1, therefore you have modulated to G major. In the consequent phrase, b, c, b, as 3, 4, 3 of the key of G, the d as 2, e as 3, d as 2 and c as 1, therefore a modulation back to C major. In Ex. 4, the c in the second measure is, at the same time, the 8th degree of the key of C and the 4th of G.

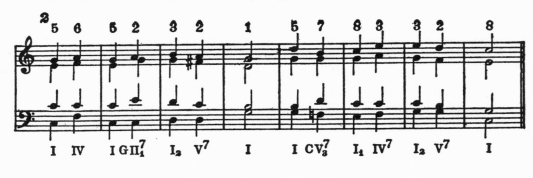

I   IV   I GII$_4^7$ I$_2$ V^7 I   I CV$_3^7$ I$_1$ IV^7 I$_2$ V^7 I

(2) *Practise the following Intervals:*

(a) Play the I, IV, II^7, II$^7_\sharp$, II$^7_{\sharp\sharp}$, V^7 and I chords in C major. Think the sound of the intervals.

(b) Play the intervals, determining their sound in relation to the root of the chord and to the key-centre.

(c) Sing the intervals.

(d) Transpose the intervals to D major.

I   II$^7_{\sharp\sharp}$ I   II^7 II^7 V^7 I VI   IV^7 V^7 I   IV^7 II^7 V^7 I   II$^7_\sharp$ II^7 V^7 I

(3)   *Exercises for Melodic Dictation and Sight-Singing:*

Modulations to the Dominant Key.   The tie in 4/4 and 6/8 meters, and skips in the II$^7_{\#\#}$ chord.

In each melody the modulation to G major is made after a I chord of C on an accented pulse.   The modulation back to C is made after the I chord of G on an accented pulse, or at the beginning of the consequent phrase.

> (a)   Play the I, V^7, I chords in C, the IV, I$_2$, V^7, I chords in G, the V^7, I chords in C.   Read the exercise mentally.
>
> (b)   Play the entire melody and decide where the modulations occur.
>
> (c)   Play the antecedent phrase twice and sing from memory to *la*.   Sing mentally the number-names, the letter-names.   Sing aloud.   Test.

NOTE.   In each melody, at the point of modulation the tones could be in either key.   A safe rule is to begin the numbers of the new key on an unaccented pulse, except after the cadence.   In the third measure of (1) the g is the 5th of c, the next three notes at first sound like 3, 2, 1 of C, but as soon as you hear the b, a, g as the 3, 2, 1 of G the mind reflects and rhythmically includes the e, d, c with the b, a, g, making it 6, 5, 4, 3, 2, 1 of G.   The next phrase begins in C.

> (d)   Practise the consequent phrase in the same way.
>
> (e)   Play the entire period and sing from memory.
>
> (f)   Transpose to the keys of B and D major.
>
> (g)   Have the melodies dictated, as outlined on page 19.

The pupil marks where the modulations occur and the scale-steps.

Section C.

(1) *Absolute Intervals.*

There are diminished 7ths in the major scale from 7–♭6, ♯2–8, ♯6–5; in the minor scale from 7–6, ♯4–3; in the ₀V♭⁹, II♯♯⁷ and VI♯♯⁷ chords. There are augmented 2nds in the major scale from ♭6–7, 8–♯2, 5–♯6; in the minor scale from 6–7, 3–♯4. A diminished 7th sounds the same as a major 6th and is sung up and down as the major 6th. The augmented 2nd sounds the same as a minor 3rd, and is sung as the minor 3rd.

(a) Sing a diminished 7th up and an augmented 2nd down from the following pitches, using first the number-names, then the letter-names. (Use the numbers 7–6 for the diminished 7th and 6–7 augmented 2nd.)

(b) Sing a diminished 7th down and an augmented 2nd up from the following pitches, using first the number-names, then the letter-names.

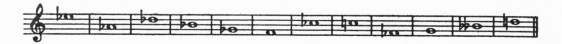

(2) *Rhythmic Drill:*

(a) Study, using the arm movement to indicate the meter, and sing to *la* on a major scale. Beat two to the measure. As the ♩. is held, the mind divides the pulse into triplets.

(3)   *Practise the following Chord Successions:*
   (a)   Sing each exercise mentally.   Test.
   (b)   Sing the number-, then the letter-names.

NOTE.   In the fourth chord of 1 the numbers are 1 3 5 8 , in the next chord the numbers are
4 6 8 4 of the key of G.

   (c)   Sing to *la,* thinking the letter- and number-names.
   (d)   From memory, i.e., write down the symbols and sing without refer-
       ence to the written exercise.
   (e)   Sing from dictation.

(f) Sing the following chord successions to the rhythm of 1: $\overset{\overset{\text{C major}}{\rule{3em}{0.4pt}}}{\text{I}, \text{IV}, \text{V}_3^7, \text{I}_1}$

$\overset{\overset{\text{G major}}{\rule{9em}{0.4pt}}}{\text{IV}_1, \text{I}_2, \text{V}_3^7, \text{I}_1, \text{IV}_\sharp^7, \text{I}_2, \text{V}^7, \text{I};}$ to the rhythm of 2: $\overset{\overset{\text{C major}}{\rule{5em}{0.4pt}}}{\text{I}, \text{III}, \text{IV}, \text{I}}$

$\overset{\overset{\text{G major}}{\rule{7em}{0.4pt}}}{\text{II}, \text{II}_\sharp^7, \text{V}^7, \text{V}_1^7, \text{I};}$ to the rhythm of 3: $\overset{\overset{\text{C major}}{\rule{9em}{0.4pt}}}{\text{I}, \text{V}_3^7, \text{I}_1, \text{II}_{\sharp\sharp}^7, \text{II}_\sharp^7, \text{II}^7, {}_0\text{V}_1^9, \text{I}}$

$\overset{\overset{\text{G major}}{\rule{9em}{0.4pt}}}{\text{IV}_1, \text{II}_2^7, \text{V}^7, \text{V}_3^7, \text{I}_1, \text{II}_{1\sharp\sharp}^7, \text{I}_2, \text{V}^7, \text{I};}$ to the rhythm of 4: $\overset{\overset{\text{C major}}{\rule{7em}{0.4pt}}}{\text{I}, \text{IV}_{2}, {}_0\text{V}^9, \text{V}_1^7, \text{I}}$

$\overset{\overset{\text{G major}}{\rule{7em}{0.4pt}}}{\text{V}^7, \text{V}_3^7, \text{I}_1, \text{IV}_\sharp^7, \text{II}_{\sharp 1}^7, \text{V}^7, \text{I}.}$

(g) Exercises for pitch and key drill. Sing the letter- and number-names. As these exercises are sung, think the entire chord as well as the tone asked for. In this way the harmonization of the tone is heard as the tone is sung.

(1) R of I in C, 3rd of I, R of IV, 3rd of IV, 5th of I, 3rd of IV in G, R of V, 7th of V^7, 3rd of V^7, R of I.

(2) 3rd of I in C, R of IV, 3rd of $\text{II}_{\sharp\sharp}^7$, R of $\text{II}_{\sharp\sharp}^7$, 3rd of I, R of V in G, 5th of V, 3rd of I, 3rd of V^7, R of I.

(3)   5th of I in C, 7th of II^7, 3rd of $II^7_{\#\#}$, 7th of V^7, 3rd of I, 5th of IV in G, 7th of II^7, 3rd of $II^7_{\#}$, 5th of V^7, 3rd of V^7, R of I.

(4)   R of I in C, 3rd of IV, 9th of the V^9, 3rd of V^7, R of I, 7th of V^7 in G, R of V^7, 3rd of V^7, R of I, 5th of V^7, R of I.

(4)   *Exercises for Sight-Singing:*

Mendelssohn

Lesson 18

Modulation to the Subdominant Key is made in the same way as to the Dominant key. Leave the key after the tonic chord on an accented pulse and begin the new key with any active chord on the unaccented pulse.

In Ex. 1 of Section B (1) the first three chords establish the key of G major. The fourth chord is the same as the third with a 7th added which immediately establishes the key of C major. In the consequent phrase the first three chords are in the key of C major; the next chord, though the same as the I of C, is the IV of G because of its resolution.

In a melody the raised 5th degree of the scale is used as a chromatic passing-tone in progressing from the 5th up to the 6th degree.

Skips are not made from the raised 5th degree. When skips are made to the raised 5th degree it resolves into the 6th degree, as it is the lower neighbor of the 6th degree.

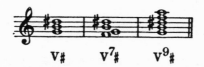

Skips may be made to or from the raised 2nd degree in the $V_\sharp$, $V_\sharp^7$, $V_\sharp^9$ chords. Skips in the I chord, or the scale-line, will follow:

$$V_\sharp \qquad V_\sharp^7 \qquad V_\sharp^9$$

Section A.

(1) Construct parallel and contrasting periods in the key of G major, modulating to the key of the subdominant and back. Employ the meter and rhythms given on pages 165 and 166. Use the $V_\sharp$, $V_\sharp^7$, and $V_\sharp^9$ chords.

Write the chord symbols and construct the melody in the usual manner.

Section B.

(1) *Practise the following Chord Successions:*

    (a) Play the entire exercise slowly, listening to the character of the chords. Do not try to think the key.

    (b) Pause after the last chord in G and think the rest of the phrase. Pause after the last chord in C and think the rest of the phrase.

    (c) Sing the number-names of the soprano as you play.

    (d) Read the exercise mentally.

(e)   Have each exercise dictated.

(1)   First playing, listen to the sound of the chords.
(2)   Second playing, write down the chord symbols.   Do not think of the keys.
(3)   Third playing, write the numbers of the scale-steps of the soprano.
(4)   Fourth playing, write the absolute pitches of the soprano.

NOTE.   In Ex. 1 the pitch b changes from the 3rd of G to the 7th of C.   In the consequent phrase, c becomes the 4th of G on account of its resolution.

(2)   *Practise the following Intervals:*

(a)   Play the I, IV, II_1^7, $II_{1\#}^7$, $II_{1\#\#}^7$, V^7 and I chords in G major.   Think the sound of the intervals.

(b)   Play the intervals, determining their sound in relation to the root of the chord and to the key-centre.

(c)   Sing the intervals.

(d)   Transpose the intervals to F major.

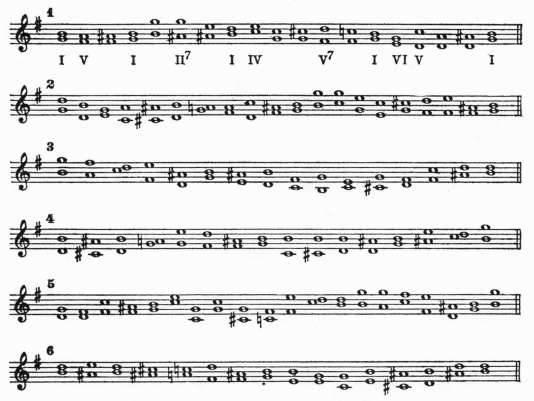

(3)   *Exercises for Melodic Dictation and Sight-Singing:*

In each melody the modulation from G to C is made after the I chord of G on the accented pulse, which becomes the V chord of C.   The modulation back to G is made in the same way or after the cadence.

(a)   Play the I, V^7, I chords in G; the V^7, I, chords in C; the IV, I_2, V^7 and I chords of G.   Read each melody mentally.

(b)   Play the entire melody and decide where the modulations occur.

(c)   Play the antecedent phrase twice and sing from memory to *la*.   Sing mentally the number-, then the letter-names.   Sing both aloud.

NOTE.   It is even harder, in modulating to the Subdominant, to decide when the modulation occurs, as the I chord of G is the V chord of C.   In (1), third measure, the high g is both the 8th degree of G and the 5th degree of C.   The f is certainly the 4th degree of C, so it is better to consider the entire pulse in C and that the numbers of g, f are 5, 4.

(d)   Practise the consequent phrase in the same way.

(e)   Play the entire period and sing from memory.

(f)   Transpose to the keys of A, F and E major.

(g)   Have the melodies dictated as outlined on page 19.

Section C.

(1) *Absolute Intervals.*

There is an augmented 5th in the major scale from 5–#2, in the minor scale from 3–7; in the V# chord in major and the III chord in minor. There is a diminished 4th in the major scale from #2–5, in the minor scale from 7–3. The augmented 5th sounds the same as the minor 6th and is sung up and down as the minor 6th. The diminished 4th sounds the same as a major 3rd, and is sung as the major 3rd.

(a) Sing an augmented 5th up and a diminished 4th down from the following pitches, using first the number-, then the letter-names.

(b) Sing a diminished 4th up and an augmented 5th down from the following pitches, using first the number-, then the letter-names.

(2) *Rhythmic Drill:*

(a) Study, using the arm movement to indicate the meter, and sing to *la* on a major scale.

(3)   *Practise the following Chord Successions:*
   (a)   Sing each exercise mentally.   Test.
   (b)   Sing the number-, then the letter-names.

NOTE.   In the fourth chord of 1, the numbers are 3 5 8 3 8 5 3; the next chord, 7 2 4 5 4 2 7 of **C** major.

   (c)   Sing to *la*, thinking the number- and letter-names.
   (d)   Sing from memory.
   (e)   Sing from dictation.

(f) Sing the following chord succession to the rhythm of 1: $\overset{\text{G major}}{I, IV_1, IV, IV_\#^7,}$

$\overset{\text{G major}}{I_2, V_\#, I}$ $\overset{\text{C major}}{V_1^7, I, II_{2\#}^7, I_2, V_\#, I;}$ to the rhythm of 2: $\overset{\text{G major}}{I, I_1, II_{\#\#}^7, II^7, V_\#, I}$

$\overset{\text{C major}}{V_3^7, V_2^7, I_1, II_{\#\#}^7, V_2^9, V_\#, I;}$ to the rhythm of 3: $\overset{\text{G major}}{I, II_2^7, II_{2\#}^7, I_2, V_\#, I}$

$\overset{\text{C major}}{V^7, V_3^7, I_1, V_\#, I;}$ to the rhythm of 4: $\overset{\text{G major}}{I, II_3^7, {}_0V^9, V_1^7, V_\#, I}$

$\overset{\text{C major}}{V_2^7, V_1^7, I, II_2^7, V_\#, I.}$

(g) Sing the exercise for pitch and key drill on page 167 in the key of G major.

(4) *Exercises for Sight-Singing:*

Handel

Lesson 19

In the double period form, the cadences at the end of the second and third phrases are often modulations to next related keys instead of semicadences in the key. When in major, at the end of the second phrase, in place of the Dominant chord, there is an authentic cadence in the Dominant Key. At the end of the third phrase, in place of the Subdominant chord, there is an authentic cadence in the Subdominant Key. After the perfect cadence in the Dominant Key, the melody must return to the original key before progressing to the Subdominant. When in minor, the second phrase modulates to the relation major key.

In a melody. the lowered 6th degree of the scale is used as a chromatic passing-

tone in progressing from the 6th down to the 5th degree.

Skips are made to and from the lowered 6th degree in the II$^7_\flat$ chord. The

scale-line, or skips in the V chord, should follow.

II$^7_\flat$

Section A.

(1) Construct parallel double periods in the key of D major, modulating to the keys of the Dominant and Subdominant. Employ the meter and rhythms given on page 176. Use the II$^7_\flat$ chord.

NOTE. Make the cadences as follows: At the end of the first phrase, an imperfect authentic cadence, or a semicadence in the key; at the end of the second phrase, an authentic cadence in the key of the Dominant; at the end of the third phrase, an authentic cadence in the key of the Subdominant; at the end of the fourth phrase, a perfect authentic cadence in the key.

Section B.

(1) *Practise the following Chord Successions:*
   (a) Play the entire exercise, listening to the character of the chords.
   (b) Pause after the last chord in D, and think the chords in A; pause after the last chord in A, and think the chords in D; pause after the last chord in D, and think the chords in G; pause after the last chord in G, and think the chords in D.

(c)   Sing the number-names of the soprano as you play the chords.

(d)   Read the exercise mentally. Test.

(e)   Have each exercise dictated as outlined on page 161.

(2)   *Practise the following Intervals:*

In the II$_b^7$ chord there will be a minor 3rd from the 3rd to the 5th of the chord, the 4th to the lowered 6th degree of the scale; a diminished 5th from the root to the 5th of the chord, the 2nd to the lowered 6th degree of the scale; a major 6th from the 5th to the 3rd of the chord, the lowered 6th to the 4th degree of the scale; an augmented 4th from the 5th to the 8th of the chord, the lowered

6th to the 2nd degree of the scale; a major 3rd from the 5th to the 7th of the chord, the lowered 6th to the 8th degree of the scale; a minor 6th from the 7th to the 5th of the chord, the 1st to the lowered 6th degree of the scale.

    (a)   Play the I, IV, II⁷, II♭⁷, V⁷ and I chords in D major. Think the sound of the intervals.

    (b)   Play the intervals, determining their sound in relation to the root of the chord and the key-centre.

    (c)   Sing the intervals.

    (d)   Transpose the intervals to C major.

(3)   *Exercises for Melodic Dictation and Sight-Singing:*

    (a)   Play the I, V⁷, I chords in D major, the IV, I₂, V⁷, I in A major, the V⁷, I in D major, the V⁷, I in G major, the II♭⁷, I₂, V⁷, I in D major. Read each melody mentally. Test.

    (b)   Play the entire melody and decide where the modulations occur.

    (c)   Play the first antecedent phrase twice. Sing from memory to *la*. Sing mentally the number-names, then use the letter-names. Sing both aloud.

    (d)   Practise the first consequent phrase in the same way.

    (e)   Play the entire first period. Sing from memory.

    (f)   Practise the second period in the same way.

    (g)   Play the entire double period and sing from memory.

    (h)   Transpose to the keys of E, C and B.

    (i)   Have the melodies dictated as outlined on page 87.

Section C.

(1)   *Rhythmic Drill.*   Syncopations in 2/4.

   (a)   Practise, using the arm movement to indicate the meter, and sing
   the rhythm to *la* on a major scale.

*This effect may be expressed   ♪♩   ♫   The tie is easier to read.

Syncopation is another term applied to irregular rhythm, the shorter notes
falling on the pulse of the meter, thus shifting the rhythmic accent. This
rhythmic variety is delightful and adds interest to a composition. In both
music and poetry, when the metric and rhythmic accent coincide, the regularity
of the pulsation is likely to grow monotonous and the mind to wander, carried
away by the regularity. What can be more comfortable than to float on in a
dreamy waltz, as in the middle section of Weber's "Invitation to the Dance"?
How often in reading poetry we find at the end of a stanza that the rhythm has
carried us on without any realization of the meaning of the words. Syncopation
disturbs this regularity; the irregularity attracts and excites us.

The long notes of any rhythm acquire stress or accent on account of their
length. When these long notes fall on the pulses of the meter, the rhythmic
and metric accent are one. When the long notes fall between the metric pulses,
both accents have to be considered. In singing and playing syncopations, a
frequent mistake is made of giving too much importance to the rhythmic accent
and thus destroying the metric accent. This is done by stressing or jumping on
the long note. As the meter is the framework upon which the composition is

hung, it must be preserved so that the listener will recognize it and in this way feel and enjoy the syncopation.

To sing this measure $\frac{2}{4}$ ♪♩ ♪ do not accent the quarter-note and

give this effect ♪♩ ♪, making it sound as if it began on the up-beat

♪ ♩ ♪ ♪ . Sing the measure with a stress on the first eighth, the metric pulse, feel the beginning of the quarter as a relaxation of that pulse, give a slight pressure as the the second pulse of the meter occurs, and feel the last eighth as a relaxation of that pulse.

(2) *Practise the following Chord Successions:*
    (a) Sing each exercise mentally. Test.
    (b) Sing the number-, then the letter-names.
    (c) Sing to *la*, thinking the number- and the letter-names.
    (d) Sing from memory.
    (e) Sing from dictation.

V_2^7 G major_____ I_____ II^7♭ D major

_____ V_2^7_____ I_____

(f) Sing the following chord successions to the rhythm of 1: I, II_3^7, $II_{3\#\#}^7$,

D major

V_1^7, I, II_b^7, V_2^7, I IV_1, V_1^7, V_3^7, I_1, II_1^7, II_{1b}^7, V^7, I V^7, V_3^7, I_1 V^7, V_3^7, I_1, $II_{\#\#}^7$, I_1

D major   A major   D major   G major

IV_1, V_1^7, V_2^7, I; to the rhythm of 2: I, IV_2, I, $_0V^9$, V_1^7, $V_\#$, I V_3^7, I_1, II_b^7,

D major   D major   A major

II_{1b}^7, I_2, V^7, I V^7, $_0V^9$, I V^7, $_0V^9$, I II, II^7, I_2, II_{2b}^7, I_2, $V_\#$, I.

A major   D major   G major   D major

(g) Exercises for pitch and key drill:
Sing the letter-, then the number-names, in the keys of D, A, and G major.

(1) R of I, R of IV, 3rd of II^7, 5th of II_b^7, R of V, 5th of $V_\#$, 3rd of I, 5th of VI, R of IV, 3rd of $II_{\#\#}^7$, 5th of I_1.

(2) 3rd of I, R of $II_{\#\#}^7$, 5th of $II_{\#\#}^7$, 5th of II^7, 5th of II_b^7, R of V, 5th of I, 3rd of V^7, 7th of V^7, 3rd of I, 5th of II_b^7, R of V, 3rd of I.

(3) 3rd of I, 5th of VI, 7th of $IV_\#^7$, 5th of $IV_\#^7$, R of $IV_\#^7$, R of $II_{\#\#}^7$, 5th of II_b^7, 7th of II_b^7, 3rd of V^7, 7th of V^7, 5th of I.

(3) *Exercises for Sight-Singing:*

Beethoven

Serly

Arr. by Serly

Folk-Song

LESSON 20

Modulation to a relative key is made after an authentic cadence, through an active chord, preferably the dominant. In Exercise 1 of Section B (1), the first chord in the second measure is the I of E♭, the next the V⁷, which resolves to the I of c minor.

In a melody skips are made to and from the lowered 6th degree in the IV⁷♭ chord. The scale-line, or skips in the II⁷♭ or V⁷ chord, should follow.

IV⁷♭

Section A.

(1) Construct periods in the key of E♭ major, modulating to the relative minor key and back. Employ the meter and rhythms given on page 185, and skips in the IV⁷♭ chord.

Section B.

(1) *Practise the following Chord Successions:*

   (a)   Play the entire exercise, listening to the character of the chords.

   (b)   Pause after the last chord in E♭ and think the chords in c minor; pause after the last chord in c minor and think the chords in E♭ major.

   (c)   Sing the number-names of the soprano as you play the chords.

   (d)   Read the entire exercise mentally.   Test.

   (e)   Have each exercise dictated as outlined on page 161.

NOTE. There will be trouble at first in hearing the numbers of the soprano, especially if the early training in music has been to sing the same numbers for the relative minor and major keys. It is only by constant practice and mental drill that this will be corrected.

(2)   *Practise the following Intervals:*

In the IV$_b^7$ chord there will be a minor 3rd from the root to the 3rd of the chord, the 4th to the lowered 6th degree of the scale; a major 3rd from the 3rd to the 5th of the chord, the lowered 6th to the 8th degree of the scale; an augmented 5th from the 3rd to the 7th of the chord, the lowered 6th to the 3rd degree of the scale; and the inversions of these intervals.

(a)   Play the I, IV^7, IV$_b^7$, II$_{1b}^7$, V^7 and I chords in E♭ major. Think the sound of the intervals.

(b)   Play the intervals, determining their sound in relation to the root of the chord and the key-centre.

(c)   Sing the intervals.

(d)   Transpose the intervals to D and F major.

(3)   *Exercises for Melodic Dictation and Sight-Singing:*

(a)   Play the I, V^7, I chords of E♭ major; the V^7, I in c minor; the VI, IV, II$_1^7$, I$_2$, V^7, I, in E♭ major. Read each exercise mentally. Test.

(b)   Play each melody, determine where the modulation occurs, and study its effect.

(c)   Play the antecedent phrase twice; sing from memory to *la*. Sing mentally the number-names, then the letter-names. Sing both aloud.

(d)   Practise the consequent phrase in the same way.

(e)   Play the entire period and sing from memory.

(f) Transpose to the keys of D, C, and F major.
(g) Have the melodies dictated as outlined on page 19.

Section C.

(1) *Rhythmic Drill.* Syncopations in 3/4 meter.

    (a)   Practise, using the arm movement to indicate the meter, and sing the rhythm to *la* on a major scale.

(2) *Practise the following Chord Successions:*

    (a)   Sing each exercise mentally.   Test for pitch.
    (b)   Sing the number-, then the letter-names.
    (c)   Sing to *la*, thinking the number- and the letter-names.
    (d)   Sing from memory.
    (e)   Sing from dictation.

NOTE.   In modulating, keep the chords common to each key in mind.

(f)   Sing the following chord successions to the rhythm of 1: $\overbrace{\text{I, II}^7, \text{II}^7_\flat, \text{V}^7_2,}^{\text{Eb major}}$

$\overbrace{\text{I, IV, IV}_\flat, \text{IV}^7_\flat, \text{I}_2, \text{V}^7, \text{I}}^{\text{Eb major}}$ $\overbrace{\text{V}^7_3, \text{I}_1, \text{II}^7, \text{V}^7_2, \text{I, IV, I}_2, \text{V}^7, \text{I}}^{\text{c minor}}$ $\overbrace{\text{V}^7_1, \text{I}}^{\text{Eb maj.}}$ $\overbrace{\text{V}^7_3, \text{I}_1}^{\text{Ab maj.}}$

$\overbrace{\text{IV}_1, \text{IV}_{1\flat}, \text{I}_2, \text{V}_\sharp, \text{I}}^{\text{Eb major}}$; to the rhythm of 2: $\overbrace{\text{I, VI, I}_2, \text{IV, IV}^7_\flat, \text{I}_2, {}_0\text{V}^9, \text{I}}^{\text{Eb major}}$

$\overbrace{\text{V}^7_2, \text{I, IV, I, V}^7_1, \text{I}}^{\text{c minor}}$ $\overbrace{\text{V}^7, {}_0\text{V}^9, \text{I}}^{\text{Eb major}}$ $\overbrace{\text{V}^7, \text{I}_1, \text{IV, IV}_\flat, \text{I}_2, \text{V}^7, \text{I}}^{\text{Ab major}}$ $\overbrace{\text{IV}^7_\flat, \text{I}_2, \text{II}^7_{2\flat},}^{\text{Eb major}}$

$\overbrace{\text{V}_7, \text{V}_\sharp, \text{I}.}^{\text{Eb major}}$

(g)   Sing the exercises for pitch and key drill on page 188 in the key of Eb major.

(3)   *Exercises for Sight-Singing:*

Brahms

LESSON 21

In a melody, skips are made to and from the lowered 6th degree in the V^9_b chord. The scale-line, or skips in the V^7 or I chord, should follow.

V^9_b

Section A.

(1) Construct periods in the key of A major, modulating to the relative minor key and back. Employ the meter and rhythms given on page 194, and skips in the V^9_b chord.

Section B.

(1) *Practise the following Chord Successions:*

   (a) Play the entire exercise, listening to the character of the chords.
   (b) Pause after the last chord in A, and think the modulatory chords to the next key; pause after the last chord in f♯, and think the chords in the next key; pause after the last chord in E and D, and think the modulatory chords to the next keys.
   (c) Sing the number-names of the soprano as you play the chords.
   (d) Read the entire exercise mentally.
   (e) Have each exercise dictated as outlined on page 161.

NOTE. In taking dictation it is good practice to take the numbers and pitches of the soprano first, the chords afterward.

(2)   *Practise the following Intervals:*

In the V_b^9 chord there will be a minor 9th from the root to the 9th of the chord, the 5th to the lowered 6th degree of the scale; a diminished 7th from the 3rd to the 9th of the chord, the 7th to the lowered 6th degree of the scale; an augmented 2nd from the 9th to the 3rd of the chord, the lowered 6th to the 7th degree of the scale; and the inversions of these intervals.

(a)   Play the I, V^7, $_0V^9$, $_0V_b^9$, V_1^7 and I chords in A major. Think the sound of the intervals.

(b)   Play the intervals, determining their sound in relation to the root of the chord and the key-centre.

(c)   Sing the intervals.

(d)   Transpose the intervals to G and B major.

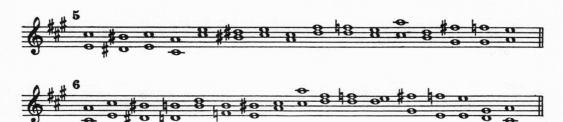

(3) *Exercises for Melodic Dictation and Sight-Singing:*

The first five melodies modulate from A major to f♯ minor. The last five from f♯ minor to A major.

- (a) Play the I, V⁷, I chords of A, V⁷, I, of f♯ minor, VI, IV, V⁹, ₀V♭⁹, I of A major. Read each exercise mentally, noting where the modulations occur.
- (b) Play the antecedent phrase twice. Sing from memory to *la*. Sing mentally the number-, then the letter-names. Sing both aloud.
- (c) Practise the consequent phrase in the same way.
- (d) Play the entire period and sing from memory.
- (e) Transpose to the keys of A, G, F, B, B♭ major.
- (f) Have the melodies dictated as outlined on page 19.

Section C.

(1) *Absolute Intervals.*

There is a minor 9th in the major scale from 5–♭6; in the minor scale from 5–6; in the V_7^9 chord. To sing a minor 9th, think a minor 2nd and sing the upper tone an octave higher.

(a) Play any tone on the piano and sing a minor 9th up, using first the number-, then the letter-names.

(b) Play any tone on the piano and sing a minor 9th down, using first the number-, then the letter-names.

(2) *Rhythmic Drill.* Syncopations in 4/4.

  (a) Practise using the arm movement to indicate the meter, and sing
       the rhythm to *la* on a major scale.

NOTE. In printed music this effect is expressed in both ways. The tie is **preferable**, as it is best **to** keep the first and third pulses clear to the eye.

(3) *Practise the following Chord Successions:*

  (a) Sing each exercise mentally.   Test for pitch.
  (b) Sing the letter-, then the number-names.
  (c) Sing to *la*, thinking the number- and the letter-names.
  (d) Sing from dictation and memory.

If there is trouble in singing the altered form of the chords, go back and sing the unaltered form two or three times.   Then sing the altered form, concentrating on the altered tones.

V^7 A major_____ I_1_____

V^7_3 f# minor_____ I_1_____ IV A major_____

$V_\#$_____ I_____

(e) Sing the following chord successions, first by letter-, then by number-names:

(1) $\overline{\text{A major}}$ I, VI, I_2, V^7_3, I_1, $II^7_{\#\#}$, I_1 $\overline{\text{E major}}$ V^7_1, $V_\#$, I, VI, $II^7_{2\flat}$, I_2, V^7, I

$\overline{\text{A major}}$ V^7_3, I_1, $II^7_\#$, V^7_2, I $\overline{\text{f\# minor}}$ V^7_3, I_1, II^7_1, I_2, V^7_1, I $\overline{\text{D maj.}}$ V^7_2, I $\overline{\text{A major}}$ II^7, $II^7_{1\flat}$, I_2, $_0V^9_\flat$, I.

(2) $\overline{\text{A major}}$ I, I_1, $IV^7_\flat$, I_2, V^7_3, I_1 $\overline{\text{E major}}$ $II^7_{2\flat}$, I_2, $_0V^9_\flat$, I $\overline{\text{A maj.}}$ V^7_2, I_1 $\overline{\text{f\# min.}}$ V^7_2, I_1 $\overline{\text{D major}}$ V^7, $V_{1\#}$, I, $II^7_{3\#\#}$, $_0V^9$, I

$\overline{\text{A major}}$ $IV^7_\flat$, I_2, $II^7_{2\flat}$, V, $V_\#$, I.

(f) Sing the exercises for pitch and key drill on page 188 in the key of A major.

(4) *Exercises for Sight-Singing:*

Schumann

Bach

Lesson 22

Modulations to keys other than the next related keys are known as *Extraneous Modulations*.

Extraneous modulations may be made by passing through the next related major and minor keys in the cycle of keys. There must be at least two chords in each key to establish the modulations. In Exercise 1 of Section B (1) the modulations are from A♭ to E♭, then to B♭, going back to A♭ through c minor. In Exercise 3 from A♭ to f minor, E♭ to g minor, B♭, E♭, and back to A♭.

In a melody, skips are made to and from the raised 4th and lowered 6th degrees in the $II^7_{2\#♭}$ chord. The scale-line, or skips in the II^7, V^7 or I_2 chord,

should follow.

Section A.

(1) Construct periods in the key of A♭ major, making extraneous modulations through the next related keys. Employ the meter and rhythms given on page 203. Use the $II^7_{2\#♭}$ chord.

Section B.

(1) *Practise the following Chord Successions:*

    (a) Play the entire exercise, listening to the character of the chords.
    (b) Pause after each modulation and think the progression into the new key. Test.
    (c) Sing the number-names of the soprano as you play the chords.
    (d) Read the entire exercise mentally.
    (e) Have each exercise dictated as outlined on page 161.

Note. Go through the exercise after it is written and see that the soprano and chords on the accented pulse are in the same key as those on the preceding unaccented pulse.

(2) *Practise the following Intervals:*

In the $II^7_{\sharp\flat}$ chord there will be an augmented 6th from the 5th to the 3rd of the chord, the lowered 6th to the raised 4th of the scale; a diminished 3rd from the 3rd to the 5th of the chord, the raised 4th to the lowered 6th degree of the scale.

(a) Play the I, II^7_2, $II^7_{2\sharp}$, $II^7_{2\sharp\flat}$, V^7 and I chords in A♭ major. Think the sound of the intervals.

(b) Play the intervals determining their sound in relation to the root of the chord and the key-centre.

(c)   Sing the intervals.
(d)   Transpose the intervals to D♭ and B♭ major.

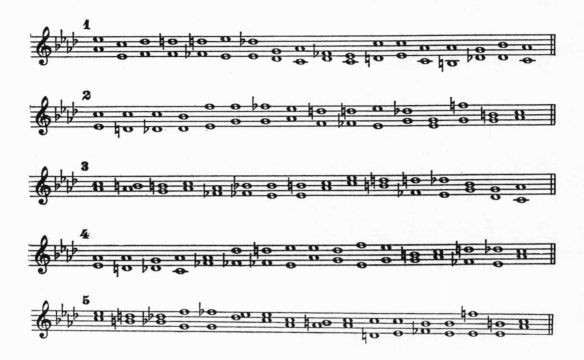

(3)   *Exercises for Melodic Dictation and Sight-Singing:*

(a)   Play the I, V⁷, I, II⁷₂♯♭, I₂, V⁷, I chords of A♭ major. Read each melody mentally, noting where each modulation occurs and the skips from ♭6 to ♯4 and ♯4 to ♭6.

(b)   In each melody sing the last four or five notes in the key before the modulation, then the first few in the new key; first to *la*, thinking the number-names, then singing the number-names. Repeat several times. For example, Melody 1. Sing the second measure and the first three notes in the third; after repeating, begin with the d♮, and sing to the cadence.

(c)   In each melody take the skips ♭6 to ♯4 and ♯4 to ♭6, and sing the 4th and 6th degrees without alteration, then in the altered form.

(d)   Play the antecedent phrase twice. Sing from memory to *la*. Sing mentally the number-, then the letter-names. Sing both aloud.

(e)   Practise the consequent phrase in the same way.

(f)   Play the entire period and sing from memory.

(g)   Transpose to the keys of A, B♭, B, C, G and F major.

(h)   Have melodies dictated as outlined on page 19.

NOTE.   While the tune is being played, relax and listen, allowing it to make an impression on the mind. Do not stop to analyze, or the context of the entire tune is lost.   Analyze after it is memorized.   In these tunes in compound meter, divide each phrase into two sections.

Section C.

(1) *Absolute Intervals.*

There are augmented 6ths in the major scale from ♭6–♯4, ♭2–7, 4–♯2; in the minor scale from 6–♯4, ♭2–7; in the II⁷♯♯♭, V⁷♭ and V⁷♯ chords. An augmented 6th sounds the same as a minor 7th, and is sung up and down as the minor 7th. There are diminished 3rds in the major scale from ♯4–♭6, 7–♭2, ♯2–4; in the minor scale, ♯4–6, 7–♭2. The diminished 3rd sounds the same as a major 2nd and is sung up and down as the major 2nd.

   (a) Sing an augmented 6th up and a diminished 3rd down from the following pitches, using first the number-, then the letter-names. Sing each, first as ♭6–♯4, determining the key of which it is a part and resolve it to the perfect 8th from 5–5; then as ♭2–7, determining the key and resolving it to the perfect 8th from 1–8.

   (b) Sing a diminished 3rd up and an augmented 6th down from the following pitches, using first the number-, then the letter-names. Sing each, first as ♯4–♭6, then as 7–♭2, determining the key and resolving each to the perfect prime 5 and 1 respectively.

(2) *Rhythmic Drill.* Syncopations in 3/4 and 4/4.

   (a) Practise using the arm movement to indicate the meter and sing the rhythm to *la* in a major scale.

NOTE. The tendency in continuous syncopation is to lose the meter. In practising these exercises, beating the meter makes it physical and you are able to think the rhythm before singing it.

(3) *Practise the following Chord Successions:*

(a) Sing each exercise mentally. Test for pitch. If you do not end in the key, go back and test after each modulation until the mistake is found. It is most important that these exercises and every interval of each chord should be thought and sung in tune.

(b) Sing the letter-, then the number-names.

(c) Sing to *la*, thinking the number- and letter-names.

(d) Sing from dictation and memory.

(e)   Sing the following chord successions, first by letter-, then by number-names, then to *la*.

$$\text{(1)} \quad \overbrace{\text{I, II}^7_{2\flat}\text{, II}^7_{2\#\flat}\text{,I}_2\text{, V}^7_3\text{, I}_1\text{,II}^7_{\#\#}}^{\text{A}\flat\text{ major}} \overbrace{{}_0\text{V}^9\text{, I}}^{\text{c min.}} \overbrace{\text{V}^7_2\text{, I}}^{\text{B}\flat\text{ maj.}} \overbrace{\text{VI,II}^7_2\text{,V}^7\text{,I}}^{\text{d minor}} \overbrace{\text{V}^7_2\text{,I}_1\text{,V}^7_1\text{, I}}^{\text{C major}} \overbrace{\text{V}^7\text{, I}}^{\text{F maj.}}$$

$$\overbrace{{}_0\text{V}^9\text{, I}}^{\text{g min.}} \overbrace{\text{V}^7_2\text{, I}}^{\text{E}\flat\text{ maj.}} \overbrace{\text{V}^7_3\text{,I}_1\text{,IV}^7_{\#}\text{,I}_2\text{, V}^7\text{, I.}}^{\text{A}\flat\text{ major}} \quad \text{(2)} \quad \overbrace{\text{I, I}_1\text{, II}^7_{\#\#}\text{,V}^7_2\text{, I, II}^7_{2\#\flat}\text{, V}^7\text{,I}}^{\text{A}\flat\text{ major}} \overbrace{\text{V}^7\text{, I}}^{\text{D}\flat\text{ maj.}}$$

$$\overbrace{\text{V}^7\text{, I}}^{\text{G}\flat\text{ maj.}} \overbrace{{}_0\text{V}^9\text{, I}}^{\text{a}\flat\text{ min.}} \overbrace{\text{V}^7\text{,V}^7_3\text{,I}_1\text{, II}^7_{\#\#}}^{\text{C}\flat\text{ major}} \overbrace{{}_0\text{V}^9\text{, I}}^{\text{e}\flat\text{ min.}} \overbrace{\text{V}^7_3\text{, I}_1}^{\text{b}\flat\text{ minor}} \overbrace{\text{IV}_1\text{,V}^7\text{,I}}^{\text{f minor}} \overbrace{\text{II}^7_{2\flat}\text{,II}^7_{2\#\flat}\text{,V}^7\text{,I.}}^{\text{A}\flat\text{ major}}$$

Think the entire chord before starting to sing it.   Always visualize on the staff.   This is difficult and requires slow and painstaking practice.   These exercises should be worked two or three times a day until they can be thought and sung with ease.

(f)   Sing the exercises for pitch and key drill on page 188 in the key of Ab major.

(3)   *Exercises for Sight-Singing:*

Lesson 23

In a melody, skips are made to and from the raised 4th, the raised 2nd and lowered 6th degree in the $II^7_{\#\#b}$ chord. The scale-line, or skips in any form of the II^7, the I and V^7 chords, should follow.

$$II^7_{\#\#b}$$

Section A.

(1) Construct double periods in the key of E major, making extraneous modulations through the next related keys. Use the $II^7_\#$, $II^7_{\#\#}$, $II^7_{2\#b}$, $II^7_{\#\#b}$, $IV^7_\#$, $_0V^9_b$, V^7 and $V_\#$ chords as a basis for the melody.

Section B.

(1) *Practise the following Chord Successions:*

(a) Play the entire exercise, listening to the character of the chords.
(b) Pause before each modulation and think the progression into the new key. Test.
(c) Sing the number-names of the soprano as you play the chords.
(d) Read the entire exercise mentally.
(e) Have each exercise dictated as outlined on page 161.

(2) *Practise the following Intervals:*

In the $II^7_{\#\#\flat}$ chord there will be a double diminished 5th from the root to the 5th of the chord, the raised 2nd to the lowered 6th degree of the scale; a double augmented 4th from the 5th to the root of the chord, the lowered 6th to the raised 2nd degree of the scale.

(a) Play the I, $II^7_{2\#}$, $II^7_{2\#\flat}$, $II^7_{2\#\#\flat}$, V^7 and I chords in E major. Think the sound of the intervals.

(b) Play the intervals, determining their sound in relation to the root of the chord and the key-centre.

(c)   Sing the intervals.

(d)   Transpose the intervals to F and D major.

(3)   *Exercises for Melodic Dictation:*

(a)   Play the I, VI, IV, IV$_{\sharp}^{7}$, I$_2$, II$^{7}_{2\sharp\sharp\flat}$, I$_2$, V$_{\sharp}$, I, chords of E major. Read each exercise mentally, noting where each modulation occurs and the skips in the II$^{7}_{\sharp\sharp\flat}$ chord.

(b)   In each melody sing the last four or five notes in the key before the modulation; then the first few in the new key; first to *la*, thinking the number-names, then singing the number-names.

NOTE. Sometimes a measure may apparently belong to either the preceding or the following key, but the context generally determines which key. In Melody 1, the first measure in the second phrase could be the V chord in either c♯ minor or E major. But as the next measure is undoubtedly the I chord in c♯ minor, it is the V chord of the same key.

(c)   In each melody take the skips in the II$^{7}_{\sharp\sharp\flat}$ chord, i.e., ♯4 to ♭6, ♯2 to ♭6, ♯2 to ♯4 to ♭6, and contrast them with the unaltered form of the chord.

(d)   Play the antecedent phrase twice. Sing from memory to *la;* sing mentally the number-, then the letter-names. Sing both aloud.

(e)   Practise the other phrases in the same way.

(f)   Transpose to the keys of A, B, C, G and F major.

(g)   Have the melody dictated as outlined on page 87.

NOTE. Do not try to remember each pitch. Reduce to chord-lines, scale-lines, single, wide and consecutive leaps. Make use of the figures, sequences.

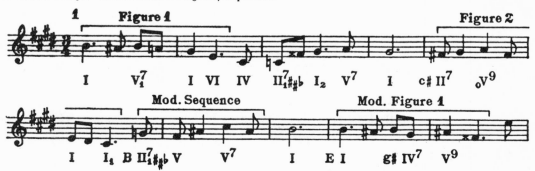

Section C.

(1)   *Absolute Intervals.*

There is a double diminished 5th in the major scale from ♯2–♭6; in the $II^7_{♯♯♭}$ and $V^9_{♯6}$ chords. The double diminished 5th sounds the same as a perfect 4th, and is sung up and down as the perfect 4th. There is a double augmented 4th in the major scale from ♭6–♯2. The double augmented 4th sounds the same as a perfect 5th, and is sung up and down as the perfect 5th.

    (a)   Sing a double diminished 5th up and a double augmented 4th down from the following pitches, using first the number-, then the letter-names.

    (b)   Sing a double augmented 4th up and a double diminished 5th down from the following pitches, using first the number-, then the letter-names.

(2)   *Rhythmic Drill.* Syncopations in 6/8 meter.

    (a)   Practise using the arm movement to indicate the meter and sing the rhythm to *la* on a major scale.

(3) *Practise the following Chord Successions:*

(a) Sing each exercise mentally. Test for pitch. Practise in a slow tempo.

(b) Sing the letter-, then the number-names.

(c) Sing to *la*, thinking the number- and letter-names.

(d) Sing from dictation. Have someone read the chord symbols to you, and sing the letter- and number-names without reference to the written exercises. Visualize the chord before singing. Use the piano for testing pitch. Never play the first note of the arpeggio until you have tried to sing it.

I_____ c♯ V_____ I

_____ E V⁷_____ I_____

(e) Sing the following chord successions, first by letter-, then by number-

names, then to *la:* (1) $\text{I, VI, II}_2^7, \text{I}_2, \text{V}_\sharp, \text{I}$ $\overbrace{}^{\text{E major}}$ $\text{V}_3^7, \text{I}_1, \text{IV}_\sharp^7, \text{I}_2, \text{V}_3^7, \text{I}_1$ $\overbrace{}^{\text{B major}}$ V_1^7, I $\overbrace{}^{\text{F♯ maj.}}$

V^7, I $\overbrace{}^{\text{C♯ maj.}}$ $_0\text{V}^9, \text{I}$ $\overbrace{}^{\text{d♯ min.}}$ V_1^7, I $\overbrace{}^{\text{g♯ min.}}$ $\text{II}^7, \text{V}^7, \text{I.}$ $\overbrace{}^{\text{E major}}$ (2) $\text{I, II}_2^7, \text{II}_{2\sharp\sharp}^7, \text{I}_2, {}_0\text{V}^9, \text{I}$ $\overbrace{}^{\text{B major}}$ $_0\text{V}^9, \text{I}$ $\overbrace{}^{\text{f♯ min.}}$ V_2^7, I $\overbrace{}^{\text{D maj.}}$

$_0\text{V}^9, \text{I}$ $\overbrace{}^{\text{e min.}}$ $\text{II}_2^7, \text{I}_2, \text{V}^7, \text{I}$ $\overbrace{}^{\text{G major}}$ V^7, I $\overbrace{}^{\text{b min.}}$ V_2^7, I $\overbrace{}^{\text{A maj.}}$ V^7, I $\overbrace{}^{\text{c♯ min.}}$ $\text{II}_1^7, \text{I}_2, \text{V}^7, \text{I.}$ $\overbrace{}^{\text{E major}}$

(4) *Exercises for Sight-Singing:*

Verdi

LESSON 24

Instead of passing through each successive key in the circle of keys when modulating to a remote key, the process may be shortened by making the I chord of any major key the V chord of a minor key, i.e., the I of C major becomes the V of f minor, thus covering four harmonic degrees.   Also the I of a minor key may be the IV♭ of a major key, i.e., the I of f minor may be treated as the IV♭ of C major.   This process of modulation is known as the *Modulatory Stride.*

C I   f V⁷   I   f I C IV♭   I₂   V   I

The distance may also be |shortened by substituting the I of the parallel

minor key when the major is expected, or the reverse.

I   V⁷   I

In a melody the raised 1st degree of the scale may be used as a passing-tone between the 1st and 2nd degrees.   Skips may be made to and from the raised 1st degree in the VI⁷♯ chord.   The scale-line, or skips in the V⁷ chord, should

follow.

VI⁷♯

Section A.

(1) Construct double periods in the key of D major, using the Stride to make extraneous modulations. Use the $VI_\sharp^7$ and the altered chords of the preceding Lessons as a basis for the melody. Employ the meter and rhythms given on page 222.

Section B.

(1) *Practise the following Chord Successions:*

(a) Play the entire exercise, listening to the character of the chords.
(b) Pause before each modulation, and think the progression into the new key.

NOTE. In Exercise (a), first phrase, instead of resolving the V chord of G in the second measure to the I chord of G major, g minor is substituted, thus covering four degrees in the circle of keys. In the second phrase, the I of g minor sounds like the IV followed by the V of d minor, while the resolution of the V is made in D major.

(c) Sing the number-names of the soprano as you play the chords.
(d) Read each exercise mentally.
(e) Have each exercise dictated as outlined on page 161.

(2) *Practise the following Intervals:*

In the VI$^7_\sharp$ chord there will be a major 3rd from the root to the 3rd of the chord, the 6th to the raised 1st degree of the scale; a minor 3rd from the 3rd to the 5th of the chord, the raised 1st to the 3rd degree of the scale; a diminished 5th from the 3rd to the 7th of the chord, the raised 1st to the 5th degree of the scale; a minor 6th from the 3rd to the 8th of the chord, the raised 1st to the 6th degree of the scale; a major 6th from the 5th to the 3rd of the chord, the 3rd to the raised 1st degree of the scale; an augmented 4th from the 7th to the 3rd of the chord, the 5th to the raised 1st degree of the scale.

   (a)   Play the I, VI$^7_{1\sharp}$, V$^7_2$, I chords in D major.   Think the sound of the intervals.
   (b)   Play the intervals, determining their sound in relation to the root of the chord and the key-centre.
   (c)   Sing the intervals.
   (d)   Transpose the intervals to E and C major.

(3) *Exercises for Melodic Dictation:*

   (a)   Play the I, VI$^7_{1\sharp}$, V$^7_2$, I chords of D major. Read each exercise mentally, noting where the modulations occur and the skips in the VI$^7_\sharp$ chord.
   (b)   In each melody sing the last four or five notes in the key before the modulation, then the first few in the new key, first to *la*, thinking the number-names, then singing the number-names.

NOTE.   The Stride is used in Melody 1 at the beginning of the third phrase which starts with the I chord of A major, which is transformed to the V chord of d minor.   Again, in the last phrase, second measure, the I chord of g minor resolves as the IV into the I of D major.

(c) Sing the skips in the VI⁷# chord, first in the unaltered form, then with the raised prime. Do the same with the skips in the other altered chords.

(d) Play the antecedent phrase twice. Sing from memory to *la;* sing mentally the number-, then the letter-names. Sing both aloud.

(e) Practise the other phrases the same way.

(f) Transpose to the keys of A, B, C, G, E and F major.

(g) Have the melody dictated as outlined on page 87.

Note. Make use of the parallel construction in memorizing the double periods.

Section C.

(1) *Rhythmic Drill.* Syncopations in 6/8 meter.

(a) Practise using the arm movement to indicate the meter and sing the rhythm to *la* on a major scale.

(2) *Practise the following Chord Successions:*
  (a) Sing each exercise mentally.   Test for pitch.
  (b) Sing the letter-, then the number-names.
  (c) Sing to *la,* thinking the number- and letter-names.
  (d) Sing from dictation.

(e) Sing the following chord successions, first by letter-, then by number-names, then to *la:*

$\overset{\text{D major}}{\mid\text{(1) I, VI}^7_{1\#}, \text{V}^7_2, \text{I, II}^7_{2\flat}, \text{II}^7_{2\#\flat}, \text{II}^7_{2\#\#\flat}, \text{I}_2, _0\text{V}^9_\flat, \text{I}}$

$\overset{\text{A major}}{\mid \text{V}^7_3, \text{I}_1,} \overset{\text{d min.}}{\mid \text{II}^7_{1\#}, \text{I}_2, \text{V}^7_3, \text{I}_1} \overset{\text{B}\flat \text{ major}}{\mid \text{V}^7_1, \text{I}} \overset{}{\mid \text{V}^7_2, \text{I, VI}^7_{1\#}, \text{V}^7_2, \text{I}_1} \overset{\text{g min.}}{\mid \text{V}^7_3, \text{I}_1} \overset{\text{D major}}{\mid \text{II}^7_{2\flat}, \text{II}^7_{2\#\#\flat}, \text{I}_2 \text{ IV}^7_\#,}$

$\overset{\text{D major}}{\mid \text{I}_2, _0\text{V}^9, \text{I.}} \quad \overset{\text{D major}}{\text{(2)} \mid \text{I, VI}^7_{1\#}, \text{V}^7_2, _0\text{V}^9_\flat, \text{I, II}^7_{3\#\#}, \text{V}^7_1, \text{I}} \overset{\text{G maj.}}{\mid \text{V}_\#, \text{I}} \overset{\text{c minor}}{\mid \text{V}^7_3, \text{I}_1, \text{II}^7_1, \text{I}_2, \text{V}^7, \text{I}}$

$\overset{\text{A}\flat \text{ major}}{\mid \text{V}^7_2, \text{I, VI}^7_{1\#}, \text{V}^7_2, \text{I}_1} \overset{\text{f min.}}{\mid \text{V}^7, \text{I}} \overset{\text{C major}}{\mid \text{IV}_\flat, \text{I}_2, \text{II}^7_{1\flat}, \text{V}^7_3, \text{I}_1} \overset{\text{e min.}}{\mid _0\text{V}^9, \text{I}} \overset{\text{D major}}{\mid \text{II}^7, \text{I}_2, \text{II}^7_{2\#\flat}, \text{V}^7, \text{V}^7_1, \text{I.}}$

(f) Exercises for pitch and key drill. Sing in all keys to number- and letter-names. Think the sound of the entire chord.

(1) 3rd of I, R of $\text{II}^7_{\#\#}$, 7th of $\text{II}^7_{\#\#}$, 3rd of V^7, 5th of $\text{V}_\#$, 3rd of I, 3rd of $\text{VI}^7_\#$, 5th of V^7, R of I, 3rd of $\text{IV}_\flat$, 7th of V^7, 3rd of I.

(2)   R of I, 3rd of VI^7, 3rd of VI$^7_\sharp$, 5th of V^7, 7th of V^7, 3rd of I,
R of II$^7_\sharp$, 3rd of II$^7_{\sharp\sharp}$, 5th of II$^7_{\sharp\sharp\flat}$, R of V, R of $_0$V^9, R of I.

(3)   *Exercises for Sight-Singing:*

Cavalli

Lewis

LESSON 25

In a melody a note which is retained by a tie, or is repeated from the preceding pulse and resolves diatonically down, rarely up, is a *suspension*. This tone is felt to be a part of the chord on the preceding pulse and to stand in place

of the tone into which it resolves.

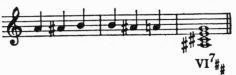

The raised 6th degree of the scale may be used as a passing-tone between the 6th and the 7th degrees, or the 7th and 6th degrees. Skips may be made to and from the raised 6th degree in the $VI^7_{\#\#}$ chord. The raised 6th degree is always used with the raised 1st degree in the VI^7 chord. The scale-line, or skips in the

V^7 chord, should follow.

Section A.

(1) Construct double periods in the key of E major, using the Stride to make extraneous modulations. Use suspensions and skips in the $VI^7_{\#\#}$ chord. Employ the meter and rhythms given on page 232.

Section B.

(1) *Practise the following Chord Successions:*

(a) Play the entire exercise, listening to the character of the chords.

(b) Pause before each modulation and think the progression into the new key.

(c) Sing the number-names of the soprano as you play the chords.

(d) Read each exercise mentally.

(e) Have each exercise dictated as outlined on page 161.

(2)   *Practise the following Intervals:*

In the VI$^7_{\#\#}$ chord, there will be a minor 3rd from the root to the 3rd of the chord, the raised 6th to the raised 1st degree of the scale; a diminished 5th from the root to the 5th of the chord, the raised 6th to the 3rd degree of the scale; a diminished 7th from the root to the 7th of the chord, the raised 6th to the 5th degree of the scale; and the inversions of these intervals.

- (a)   Play the I, VI^7, VI$^7_{\#}$, VI$^7_{\#\#}$, V$^7_1$, I chords in E major. Think the sound of the intervals.
- (b)   Play the intervals, determining their sound in relation to the root of the chord and the key-centre.
- (c)   Sing the intervals.
- (d)   Transpose the intervals to F and D major.

NOTE.   If there is trouble in hearing the intervals formed by the altered tones, contrast them with the intervals formed by the same scale steps unaltered.

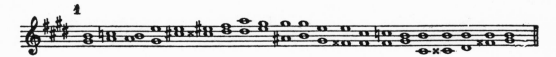

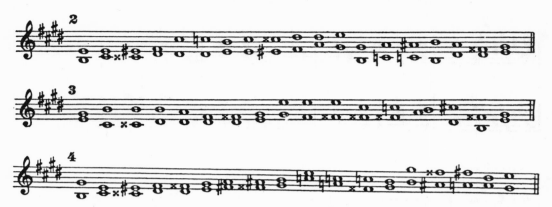

(3)   *Exercises for Melodic Dictation:*

  (a)   Play the I, VI⁷##, V⁷₁, I, II⁷₂#♭, V⁷, I chords in E major. Read each exercise mentally, noting where the modulations occur and the use of the VI⁷## chord.

  (b)   In each melody sing the last four or five notes in the key before the modulation, then the first few in the new key, first to *la*, thinking the number-names, then singing the number-names.

  (c)   Sing the skips in the VI⁷## chord, first in the unaltered form, then with the raised 6th and 1st degrees. Do the same with the skips in the other altered chords.

  (d)   Note the suspensions and sing the two tones that make the suspension, first without the tie, i.e., placing the second tone on the accent, then as written. Contrast several times until the effect is mentally grasped.

  (e)   Play the antecedent phrase twice. Sing from memory to *la*, sing mentally the number-, then the letter-names. Sing both aloud.

  (f)   Practise the other phrases in the same way.

  (g)   Transpose to the keys of A, D, G, C and F major.

  (h)   Have the melody dictated as outlined on page 87.

NOTE. In these 6/8 syncopations, keep the pulse clearly in mind. As you read or think the tune, beat the meter, using the arm movements, down, up.

Section C.

(1) *Rhythmic Drill.*　The tie in 2/4 and 3/4 meter.

(a) Practise using the arm movement to indicate the meter, and sing the rhythm to *la* in a major scale.

Note.　In singing a tied note over the bar, a slight **crescendo is made up** to the note, and a pressure given on the note, so as to preserve the metric accent.

(2) *Practise the following Chord Successions:*

(a) Sing each exercise mentally at a slow tempo.
(b) Sing the letter-, then the number-names.
(c) Sing to *la*, thinking the number- and the letter-names.
(d) Sing from dictation.

Note.　Work carefully for correct intonation.

(e)   Sing the following chord successions, first by letter-, then by number-

names, then to *la:* (1) $\overline{\text{I, VI, VI}^7_{\#\#}, \text{V}^7_1, \text{I}}$ $\overline{_0\text{V}^9, \text{I, II}^7_2, \text{I}_2, \text{V}^7_3, \text{I}_1}$ $_0\text{V}^9, \text{I}$

(over brackets: E major | f# minor | B maj.)

$\overline{\text{V}^7, \text{I, VI}}$ $\overline{\text{II}^7_{1b}, \text{I}_2, \text{V}^7_3, \text{I}_1}$ $\overline{\text{II}^7_{2b}, \text{II}^7_{2\#b}, \text{I}_2, \text{V}_\#, \text{I.}}$ (2) $\overline{\text{I, V}^7_2, \text{VI}^7_{1\#\#}, \text{V}^7_2, \text{I}}$

(over brackets: e minor | G major | E major | E major)

$\overline{\text{V}^7_3, \text{I}_1}$ $\overline{\text{II}^7_{1\#\#}, \text{I}_2}$ $\overline{\text{V}^7_3, \text{I}_1}$ $\overline{\text{II}^7_{2b}, \text{II}^7_{2\#b}, \text{V}^7, \text{I}}$ $_0\text{V}^9, \overline{\text{I}}$ $\overline{\text{II}^7_{1b}, \text{V}^7_3, \text{I}_1, \text{V}^7_2, \text{VI}^7_{1\#\#}, \text{V}^7_2, \text{I}}$

(over brackets: a min. | G major | g min. | D major | d min. | A major)

$\overline{\text{IV}_b, \text{I}_2, \text{II}^7_{2\#b}, \text{V}^7, \text{I.}}$

(over bracket: E major)

(3)   *Exercises for Sight-Singing:*

LESSON 26

Abrupt modulations to remote keys may be made at any time after a cadence and in the sequence of a figure. These are known as *Cadential* and *Sequential*

Modulations.   In all modulations it is best to have common tones.   In Exercise 1, Section B (1), first phrase, after the cadence in B, the next chord is the I of G.   This sounds well, because of the common tone B.   In Exercise 3 there is a repetition in b minor of the first three chords.   In Exercise 2 there is a repetition in minor of the first two chords, then an abrupt modulation to C major, keeping the same soprano, then a modulation back to B, through e minor, using the Stride.   In Exercise 4 there is an abrupt modulation to D major, making the 1st degree of B the 6th of D; then a modulation to b minor and a cadence in B major.

A Diminished Seventh-Chord is a seventh-chord, all the tones of which are a minor third apart.   In each major key, there are two: $_0V^9$ chord, and the $IV^7_{\#\flat}$ chord:

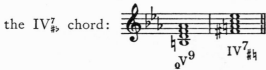

The diminished seventh-chord is most useful in modulating, as each chord may be spelled in four or five ways and resolved as a $_0V^9_\flat$, $II^7_{\#\#}$, $VI^7_{\#\#}$ or $IV^7_{\#\natural}$ chord.

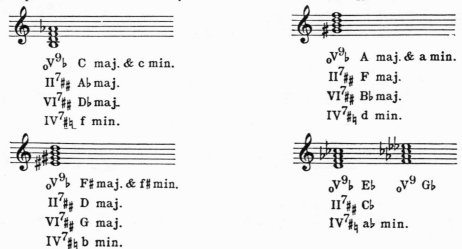

$_0V^9_\flat$ C maj. & c min.
$II^7_{\#\#}$ Ab maj.
$VI^7_{\#\#}$ Db maj.
$IV^7_{\#\natural}$ f min.

$_0V^9_\flat$ A maj. & a min.
$II^7_{\#\#}$ F maj.
$VI^7_{\#\#}$ Bb maj.
$IV^7_{\#\natural}$ d min.

$_0V^9_\flat$ F# maj. & f# min.
$II^7_{\#\#}$ D maj.
$VI^7_{\#\#}$ G maj.
$IV^7_{\#\natural}$ b min.

$_0V^9_\flat$ Eb $_0V^9$ Gb
$II^7_{\#\#}$ Cb
$IV^7_{\#\natural}$ ab min.

Section A.

(1)   Construct double periods in the key of B major, using cadential and sequential modulations to remote keys.   Use suspensions and skips in the diminished seventh-chords.   Embellish the tones of the chord by jumping from the lower to the upper, or from the upper to the lower neighbors.   Employ the meter and rhythms given on page 242.

Section B.

(1)   *Practise the following Chord Successions:*

    (a)   Play the entire exercise, listening to the character of the chords.

    (b)   Pause before each modulation, and think the progression into the new key.

    (c)   Sing the number-names of the soprano as you play the chords.

    (d)   Read each exercise mentally.

    (e)   Have each exercise dictated as outlined on page 161.

NOTE.   In taking down the chord symbols, do not try to analyze the keys.   Write down the symbols of the chords as you hear them, and determine the keys from the soprano.

(2) *Practise the following Intervals:*

(a) Play the I, V⁷, I chords in B major. Think the sound of the intervals.
(b) Play the intervals, determining their sound in relation to the root of the chord and the key-centre.
(c) Sing the intervals.
(d) Transpose the intervals to C and A major.

(3)   *Exercises for Melodic Dictation:*

(a)   Play the I, VI$^7_{\#\#}$, V$^7_1$, I, II$^7_{2\#\flat}$, I$_2$, V$_\#$, I chords in B major.   Read each exercise mentally, noting where the modulations occur and how they are made.

In Melody 1, the end of the second phrase is an authentic cadence in F♯ major; the next phrase begins with the tonic chord of D major without any introduction, but keeping the common tone F sharp.   In Melody 4, the first section of the third phrase is a figure in G major, the second section a sequence of this figure in E major.

(b)   In each melody, sing the last four or five notes in the key before the modulation, then the first few in the new key, first to *la*, thinking the number-names, then singing the number-names.   Where the modulations are made in sequence, sing the entire figure.

(c)   Note the suspensions and the neighboring notes.

(d)   Play the antecedent phrase twice.   Sing from memory to *la*.   Sing mentally the number-, then the letter-names.   Sing both aloud.

(e)   Practise the other phrases in the same way.

(f)   Transpose to the keys of A, G and C major.

(g)   Have the melody dictated as outlined on page 87.

Note.   In these abrupt modulations, determine the number-name of the pitch first, then the letter-name.

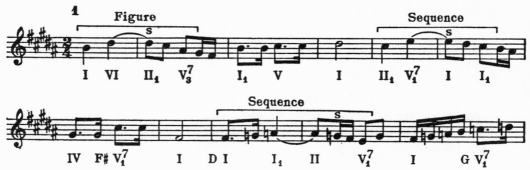

(1) *Rhythmic Drill.* The tie in 4/4 meter.

    (a) Practise, using the arm movement to indicate the meter. Sing the rhythm to *la* on a major scale.

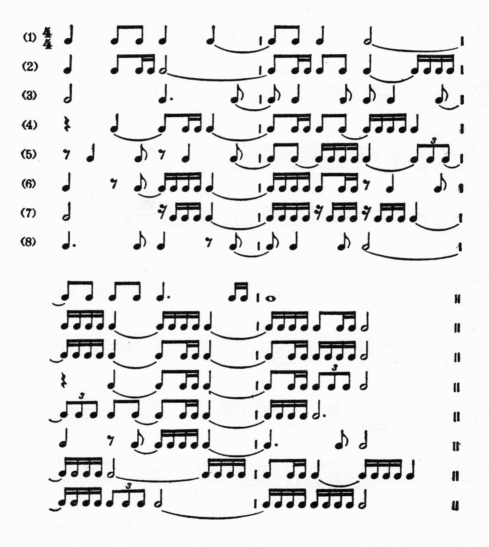

(2) *Practise the following Chord Successions:*

    (a) Sing each exercise mentally.
    (b) Sing the letter-, then the number-names.
    (c) Sing to *la*, thinking the number- and the letter-names.
    (d) Sing from dictation.

(e) Sing the following chord successions, first by letter-, then by number-

names, then to *la:* (1) I, II$_{3\#\#}^7$, V$_1^7$, I, VI$_{1\#\#}^7$, V$_2^7$, I | V$_2^7$, I | V^7, I | V^7, I

V^7,   I | IV$_{1b}$, I$_2$, V^7, I | IV$_{1b}$, I$_2$, V^7, I.   (2) I, VI, VI$_{\#\#}^7$, V$_1^7$, I | I, VI$_{1\#\#}^7$, V$_2^7$, I

I, VI$_{1\#\#}^7$, V$_2^7$, I | I, V$_2^7$, I$_1$ | II$_{2b}^7$, I$_2$, V$_1^7$, I | V$_2^7$, I | IV$_{1b}$, I$_2$, V$_1^7$, I.

(3)　*Exercises for Sight-Singing:*

LESSON 27

When a tone on the last half of the pulse is repeated, anticipating the tone on the first half of the next pulse, it is an *Anticipation*. An Anticipation is

generally a short note.

The lowered 2nd degree of the scale is used as a chromatic passing-tone from the 2nd degree to the 1st degree of the scale. Skips may be made to and from the lowered 2nd degree in the $V_{2\flat}^7$ chord. Scale-line, or skips in the I chord,

should follow.

Section A.

(1) Construct double periods in the key of F major, using cadential and sequential modulations to remote keys. Use anticipations, suspensions and skips in the $V_{2\flat}^7$ chord. Employ the meter and rhythms given on page 252.

Section B.

(1) *Practise the following Chord Successions:*
  (a) Play the entire exercise, listening to the character of the chords.
  (b) Pause before each modulation and think the progression into the new key.
  (c) Sing the number-names of the soprano as you play the chords.
  (e) Have each exercise dictated as outlined on page 161.

(2)   *Practise the following Intervals:*

In the V_{2b}^7 chord, there will be a major 3rd, from the 5th to the 7th of the chord, the lowered 2nd to the 4th degree of the scale; an augmented 4th from the 5th to the root of the chord, the lowered 2nd to the 5th degree of the scale; an augmented 6th from the 5th to the 3rd of the chord, the lowered 2nd to the 7th degree of the scale.

- (a)   Play the I, V_2^7, V_{2b}^7, I chords in F major.   Think the sound of the intervals.
- (b)   Play the intervals, determining their sound in relation to the root of the chord and the key-centre.
- (c)   Sing the intervals.
- (d)   Transpose the intervals to E and G major.

(3) *Exercises for Melodic Dictation:*

(a) Play the I, V_1^7, I, $II_{2\#\#}^7$, $II_{2\#\#\flat}^7$, I_2, V_2^7, $V_{2\flat}^7$, I chords in F major, and read the exercises mentally, noting the modulations, suspensions and anticipations.

(b) In each melody sing the last four or five notes in the key before the modulation, then the first few in the new key, first to *la*, thinking the number-names, then singing the number-names.

(c) Sing the tones which make the suspension, first without the suspension, then as written.   Practise the anticipation in the same way.

(d) Play the antecedent phrase twice.   Sing from memory to *la*.   Sing mentally the number-names, then the letter-names.   Sing both aloud.

(e) Practise the other phrases in the same way.

(f) Transpose to the keys of B, A, E, D and G major.

(g) Have each melody dictated as outlined on page 87.

NOTE.   Divide the phrases into two sections.   Have the entire phrase dictated, because the phrase is a complete thought and must be grasped as such.

Section C.

(1) *Rhythmic Drill.* The tie in 6/8 meter.

(a) Practise, using the arm movement to indicate the meter. Sing the rhythm to *la* on a major scale.

NOTE. Use the arm movement two pulses to a measure. The mind subdivides each pulse into triplets. In singing make the metric pulse clear to the listener by pressure on the tied note. This effect can also be made on the violin by an added pressure of the bow. On the piano this is not possible, but the pianist will find that his playing is much more rhythmic, therefore interesting, if he makes the effect mentally.

(2) *Practise the following Chord Successions:*

(a) Sing each exercise mentally.
(b) Sing the letter-, then the number-names.
(c) Sing to *la*, thinking the number-, and the letter-names.
(d) Sing from dictation.

(e) Sing the following chord successions, first by letter-, then by number-names, then to *la:* (1) I, V_{2b}^7, I, $II_{2\#\#}^7$, $II_{2\#\#b}^7$, I_2, $_0V_b^9$, I | V^7, I | V^7, I F major | D maj. | Bb maj

V^7, I | I,$_0V_b^9$I, | I,$_0V_b^9$,I,I_1 | $_0V_b^9$, I, V_{2b}^7, I, $II_{2\#b}^7$,V^7,I. (2) $I,VI_{1\#\#}^7,V_2^7,V_{2b}^7,$I G maj. | E major | C major | F major | F major

I,V_{2b}^7,I | I,V_2^7,I | $II_b^7,V_2^7,V_{2b}^7,$I | V^7, I | V^7, I | V^7, I | $IV_b,I_2,V_\#,$I. Db major | bb min. | F major | G maj. | A maj. | Bb maj. | F major

(3) *Exercises for Sight-Singing:*

Wagner

LESSON 28

Abrupt modulations to remote keys may be made at any point by a chromatic progression. The chromatic progression may be in any part, but is best in the soprano or the bass. This is known as *Chromatic Modulation*. In Exercise 2 of Section B (1), first phrase, the chromatic inflection is in the bass; in the second phrase, in the soprano. Chromatic modulation is one form of Sequential Modulation.

Abrupt modulations may also be made by enharmonically changing the pitch of a tone. This is known as *Enharmonic Modulation*. In Exercise 1 the pitch Ab, the fifth of the key of Db major, becomes G#, the 7th degree of a minor.

In a melody, skips may be made to and from the lowered 2nd degree of the scale in the II♭♭ chord with the lowered 6th degree. Scale-line or skips in the

V⁷ chord should follow.

II♭♭

Section A.

(1) Construct double periods in the key of C major, using chromatic and enharmonic modulations to remote keys. Use anticipations, suspensions and skips in the II♭♭ chord. Employ the meter and rhythms given on page 262.

NOTE. The chromatic inflection in a melody may often be either a modulation or an altered tone in the key, the modulation being determined by the harmonization.

Section B.

(1) *Practise the following Chord Successions:*

(a) Play the entire exercise, listening to the character of the chords.
(b) Pause before each modulation and think the progression into the new key.
(c) Sing the number-names of the soprano as you play the chords.
(d) Have each exercise dictated as outlined on page 161.

NOTE. In Exercise 1, fifth measure, you hear that the Ab has become G#, because Ab could not be the 7th degree of the scale. In Exercises 2 and 3 the key of Cb could have been used in the place of B.

(2)   *Practise the following Intervals:*

In the II♭♭ chord there will be a major 3rd from the root to the 3rd of the chord, the lowered 2nd to the 4th degree of the scale; a perfect 5th from the root to the 5th of the chord, the lowered 2nd to the lowered 6th degree of the scale; and the inversions of these intervals.

   (a)   Play the I, IV, II, II♭♭, V$_2^7$ and I chords in the key of C major. Think the sound of the intervals.
   (b)   Play the intervals, determining their sound in relation to the root of the chord and the key-centre.
   (c)   Sing the intervals.
   (d)   Transpose the intervals to F, D and B major.

(3) *Exercises for Melodic Dictation:*

- (a) Play the I, V⁷, I, II♭, II♭♭, V⁷₂♭, I chords in the key of C major, **and** read the exercises mentally, noting the modulations, suspensions and anticipations.

- (b) In each melody sing the last few notes in the key before the modulation, then the first few in the new key, first to *la*, thinking the number-names, then singing the number-names.

- (c) Sing the tones which make the suspension, first without the suspension, then as written. Practise the anticipation in the same way.

- (d) Play the antecedent phrase twice, sing from memory to *la*. Sing mentally the number-names, then use the letter-names. Sing both aloud.

- (e) Practise the other phrases in the same way.

- (f) Transpose to other major keys.

- (g) Have each melody dictated as outlined on page 87.

Section C.

(1) *Rhythmic Drill.* Review. Rhythms from Bach.

   (a) Practise using the arm movement to indicate the meter. Sing the rhythm to *la* on a major scale.

(2) *Practise the following Chord Successions:*

    (a)   Sing each exercise mentally.
    (b)   Sing the letter-, then the number-names.
    (c)   Sing to *la*, thinking the number- and the letter-names.
    (d)   Sing from dictation.

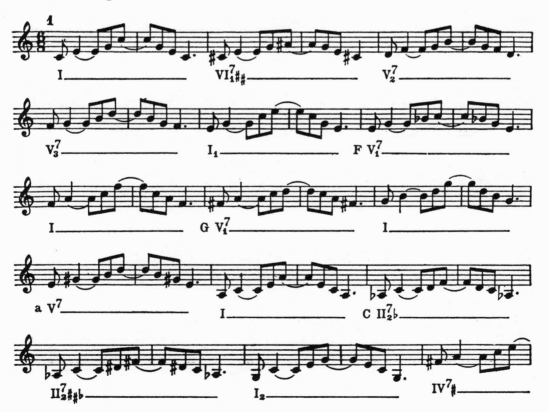

(e) Sing the following chord successions, first by letter-, then by number-names, then to *la:*

(1) C major: $I, IV, II_{1bb}, V_3^7, I_1, V_{2b}^7, I$ | D maj.: V_1^7, I | E maj.: V_1^7, I | F# maj.: V_1^7, I | b min.: V^7, I | C major: $V^7, I, I_1, II_{1bb}, I_2, V^7, I.$

(2) C major: $I, II_{1b}^7, I_1, II_{1bb}, I_{1,0}V^9, I$ | Db maj.: $_0V_b^9$ | C maj.: $_0V_b^9$ | B maj.: $_0V_b^9$ | Bb maj.: $_0V_b^9, I$ | C maj.: V_1^7, I | d min.: V_1^7, I | C major: $V_{2b}^7, I, IV, II_{1bb}, I_2, V^7, I.$

(3) *Exercises for Sight-Singing:*

Brahms

LESSON 29

In a melody, skips are often made from above to the lower neighbor of a tone, or from below to the upper neighbor of a tone. An entire arpeggio may be embellished in this way, as the B♭ chord in the sixth measure of Melody 3, Section B (3). The neighbor generally resolves immediately to the tone, though it may jump to the other neighbor before resolving, as in the first measure of Melody 3, Section B (3).

Skips may be made to and from the lowered 2nd degree of the scale in the $_0V^9_{♭♭}$ chord with the lowered 6th degree. Scale-line or skips in the V^7 chord should follow.

Section A.

(1) Construct double periods in the key of D major, using all types of modulations to next related and remote keys. Use anticipations, suspensions and skips in the $_0V^9_{\flat\flat}$ chord. Embellish tones by jumping to the neighbors. Employ the meter and rhythms given on pages 270-271.

Section B.

(1) *Practise the following Chord Successions:*

  (a) Play the entire exercise, listening to the character of the chords.
  (b) Pause before each modulation and think the progression into the
       new key.
  (c) Sing the number-names of the soprano as you play the chords.
  (d) Have each exercise dictated as outlined on page 161.

$$I \quad V^7_3 \quad I_1 F_0 V^9 \quad I_1 B\flat V^7 \quad I \quad D\flat_0 V^9_1 \quad V^7_1 \quad I \quad I \quad D V^7 \quad V^7_1 \quad I$$

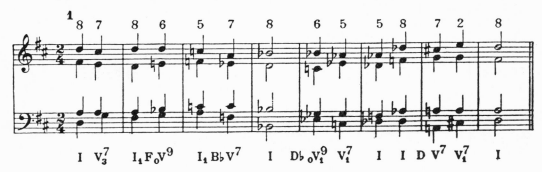

(2) *Practise the following Intervals:*

The same intervals will be found in the $_0V^9_{\flat\flat}$ chord as in the $II_{\flat\flat}$ chord.

  (a) Play the I, IV, II_1, $II_{1\flat\flat}$, $_0V^9_{\flat\flat}$, $V^7_{2\flat}$, and I chords in the key of
       D major. Think the sound of the intervals.

(b) Play the intervals, determining their sound in relation to the root of the chord and the key-centre.

(c) Sing the intervals.

(d) Transpose the intervals to other major keys.

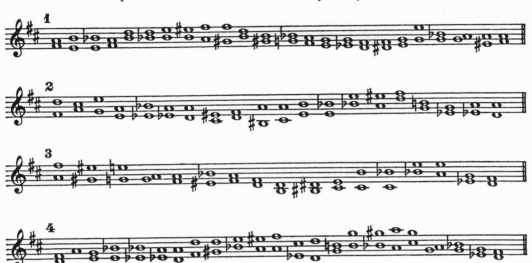

(3) *Exercises for Melodic Dictation:*

(a) Play the I, V_3^7, I_1, IV, $II_{1\flat\flat}$, I_2, V^7 and I chords in the key of D major. Read each exercise mentally, noting the modulations, suspensions, anticipations and neighboring tones.

(b) Sing the last few notes in the key before the modulation, then the first few in the new key, first to *la*, thinking the number-names, then singing the number-names.

(c) Sing the measures which have skips in the $II_{\flat\flat}$ chord. Contrast the altered and unaltered forms of this arpeggio.

(d) Play the antecedent phrase twice, sing from memory to *la*; sing mentally the number-, then the letter-names. Sing both aloud.

(e) Practise the other phrases in the same way.

(f) Transpose to other major keys.

(g) Have each melody dictated as outlined on page 87.

Section C.

(1) *Rhythmic Drill.*   Regular Rhythm in 9/8 meter.

(a) Practise using the arm movement to indicate the meter. Sing the rhythm to *la* on a major scale. In 9/8 meter use the same arm movement as for triple meter, and mentally subdivide each pulse into triplets. All of the rhythmic figures used in 6/8 are found in 9/8 meter.

(2) *Practise the following Chord Successions:*

 (a) Sing each exercise mentally.
 (b) Sing the letter-, then the number-names.
 (c) Sing to *la*, thinking the number- and the letter-names.
 (d) Sing from dictation.

NOTE. Sing the chords that are enharmonically changed, with both spellings and resolutions. **Work** carefully for correct intonation, as these exercises serve no purpose unless sung perfectly in tune.

(e) Sing the following chord successions, first by letter-, then by number-names, then to *la:* (1) $I, {_0}V^9_{b}, {_0}V^9_{1b}, {_0}V^9_{1bb}, V^7_2, I, VI^7_{1\#\#}$ ⎰D major⎱ ${_0}V^9_{b}, I, II^7_{2\#\#}, I_2$ ⎰F major⎱ $II^7_{1\#\#}, I_2$ ⎰F major⎱ ${_0}V^9_{b}, V^7, I.$ ⎰D major⎱ (2) $I, II^7_{3b}, {_0}V^9_{b}, I, VI^7, VI^7_{\#\#}, {_0}V^9_{b}, I$ ⎰D major⎱ ${_0}V^9_{b}, I$ ⎰Db maj.⎱ V^7_3, I_1 ⎰Gb maj.⎱ ${_0}V^9_{b}, I$ ⎰Bb maj.⎱ $II^7_{2\#b}, I_2, V^7, I.$ ⎰D major⎱

(3) *Exercises for Sight-Singing:*

Foster

Cowen

Lesson 30

Abrupt modulations may be made to any key by retaining and using as a pivot a tone common to both keys. This is known as *Pivotal Modulation*. In Exercise 1, Section B (1), the 1st degree of c minor becomes the 4th of G major; the 3rd degree of G major becomes the 5th of E major. In Exercise 2 the C in the soprano, the 8th degree in c minor, becomes the leading-tone of Db; the Db in the soprano, the 1st degree of Db, enharmonically changes to C♯ and becomes the 7th degree of d minor.

In minor the 6th degree is raised in the ascending form of the melodic scale,

and is harmonized by the II♭, II♭⁷, IV♭ or IV♭⁷ chords.

Section A.

(1) Construct double periods in c minor, using pivotal and all other types of modulation to next related and remote keys. Use anticipations, suspensions, and skips in chords embellished by jumping to the neighbors. Employ the meter and rhythms given on page 279.

Section B.

(1) *Practise the following Chord Successions:*
    (a) Play the entire exercise, listening to the character of the chords and modulations.

(b) Pause before each modulation and think the progression into the new key.

(c) Sing the number-names of the soprano as you play the chords.

(d) Have each exercise dictated as outlined on page 161.

(2) *Practise the following Intervals:*

(a) Play the I, IV$_{\natural}$, II$_{\natural}$, V^7 and I chords in the key of **c** minor. Think the sound of the intervals.

(b) Play the intervals, determining their sound in relation to the root
     of the chord and the key-centre. Note the altered intervals
     resulting from the melodic form of the scale.

(c) Sing the intervals.

(d) Transpose the intervals to other minor keys.

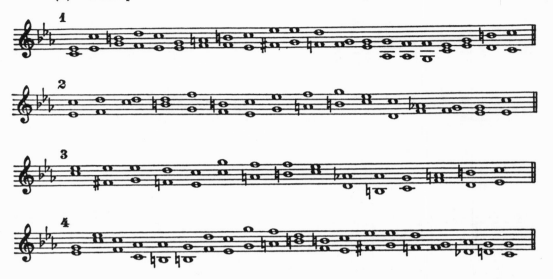

(3) *Exercises for Melodic Dictation:*

(a) Play the I, V^7, I, IV, II^7_4, V^7 and I chords in the key of c minor.
     Read each exercise mentally, noting the modulations and embel-
     lishments.

(b) Sing the last few notes in the key before the modulation, then the
     first few in the new key, first to *la*, thinking the number-names,
     then singing the number-names.

(c) Play the antecedent phrase twice, sing from memory to *la*. Sing
     mentally the number-, then the letter-names. Sing both aloud.

(d) Practise the other phrases in the same way.

(e) Transpose to other minor keys.

(f) Have each melody dictated as outlined on page 87.

(1). *Rhythmic Drill.* Irregular Rhythm in 9/8 meter.
    (a) Practise using the arm movement to indicate the meter. Sing the rhythm to *la*, on a major scale.

(2) *Practise the following Chord Successions:*
    (a) Sing each exercise mentally.
    (b) Sing the letter, then the number-names.
    (c) Sing to *la*, thinking the number- and letter-names.
    (d) Sing from dictation.

(e)   Sing the following chord successions, first by letter-, then by number-names, then to *la*: (1) I, II$_1^7$, V$_3^7$, I$_1$, II$_{1\natural}^7$, V, I | $\overbrace{}^{\text{c minor}}$ V^7, I | $\overbrace{}^{\text{Db maj.}}$ V$_1^7$, I | $\overbrace{}^{\text{D maj.}}$ $_0$V$_b^9$, I | $\overbrace{}^{\text{Eb maj.}}$

$_0$V^9, I | $\overbrace{}^{\text{f minor}}$ II$_1^7$, II$_2^7$, I$_2$, II$_{1\natural}^7$, V^7, I. | $\overbrace{}^{\text{c minor}}$ (2) I, IV^7, II$_1^7$, II$_{1\natural}^7$, I$_2$, $_0$V$_2^9$ | $\overbrace{}^{\text{c minor}}$ $_0$V$_{3b}^9$, I$_2$ | $\overbrace{}^{\text{A maj.}}$

$_0$V$_1^9$, I | $\overbrace{}^{\text{E maj.}}$ $_0$V$_b^9$, I | $\overbrace{}^{\text{D maj.}}$ II$_\natural^7$, V$_2^7$, I. | $\overbrace{}^{\text{c minor}}$

(3)   *Exercises for Sight-Singing:*

Bach

Spohr

LESSON 31

Section A.

(1) Construct double periods in e minor, using all types of modulation to next related and remote keys. Use all embellishments, and employ the meter and rhythms given on page 288.

Section B.

(1) *Practise the following Chord Successions:*

(a) Play the entire exercise, listening to the character of the chords and modulations.

(b) Pause before each modulation and think the progression into the new key.

(c) Sing the number-names of the soprano as you play the chords.

(d) Have each exercise dictated as outlined on page 161.

(2)   *Practise the following Intervals:*

  (a)   Play the I, IV, II₁, V²₂ and I chords in the key of e minor.   Think
         the sound of the intervals.
  (b)   Play the intervals, determining their sound in relation to the root
         of the chords and the key-centre.
  (c)   Sing the intervals.
  (d)   Transpose the intervals to other minor keys.

(3)   *Exercises for Melodic Dictation:*

  (a)   Play the I, IV♮, II⁷₁♮, I₂, V⁷ and I chords in the key of e minor.   Read
         each exercise mentally, noting the modulations and embellish-
         ments.
  (b)   Sing the last few notes in the key before the modulation, then the
         first few in the new key, first to *la*, thinking the number-names,
         then singing the number-names.
  (c)   Play the antecedent phrase twice.   Sing from memory to *la*.   Sing
         mentally the number-names, then use the letter-names.   Sing both
         aloud.
  (d)   Practise the other phrases in the same way.
  (e)   Transpose to other minor keys.
  (f)   Have each melody dictated as outlined on page 87.

Section C.

(1) *Rhythmic Drill.* Regular Rhythm in 12/8 meter.

(a) Practise using the arm movement to indicate the meter. Sing the rhythm to *la* on a major scale. In 12/8 meter use the same arm movement as for quadruple meter and mentally subdivide each pulse into triplets. All the rhythmic figures used in 6/8 are found in 12/8 meter.

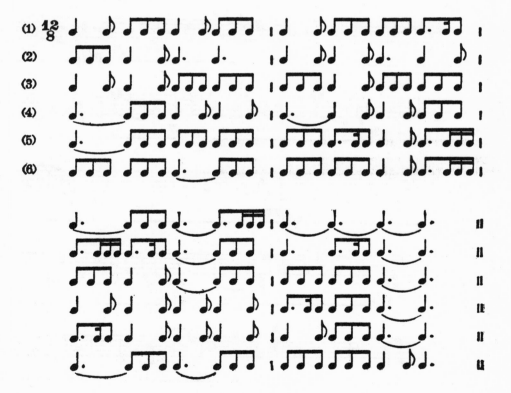

(2) *Practise the following Chord Successions:*
(a) Sing each exercise mentally.
(b) Sing the letter-names, then use the number-names.
(c) Sing to *la*, thinking the number- and letter-names.
(d) Sing from dictation.

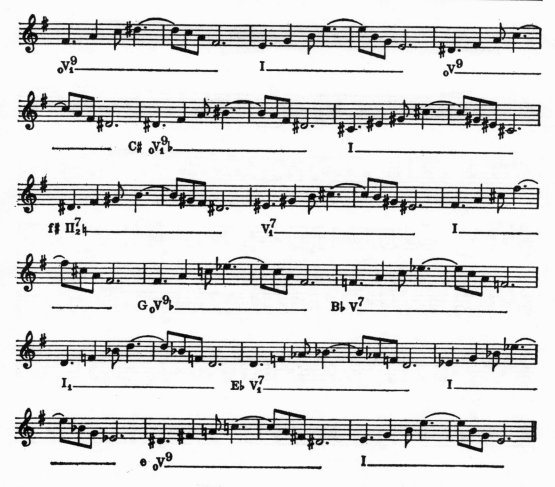

(e) Sing the following chord successions, first by letter-, then by number-names, then to *la*: (1) I, VI, II_2^7, I_2, $II_{2\natural}^7$, V_1^7, I $\overbrace{V_2^7, I}^{\text{C maj.}}$ $\overbrace{V_2^7, I}^{\text{A}\flat\text{ maj.}}$ $\overbrace{V_{2\flat}^7, I}^{\text{G maj.}}$

V, I, $II_{2\natural}^7$, V_1^7, I. (2) I, II_3^7, $_0V^9$, I $_0V_\flat^9$, I $\overbrace{V_1^7, I, II_{2\natural}^7, V_1^7, I}^{\text{c}\sharp\text{ minor}}$ $_0V_\flat^9$, I

$_0V_\flat^9$, I, II_2^7, I_2, $II_{2\natural}^7$, V_1^7, I.

(3) *Exercises for Sight-Singing:*

Mackenzie

LESSON 32

A composition often divides into sections which vary in length from a phrase to a double period or a series of phrases. These sections are known as *Parts*. When two of these parts are used, the second answering and a complement of the first part, the form is known as a *Two-Part Song-Form*. The parts of a Two-part Song-form may be of any length, though rarely shorter than a period, and more often a double period. The cadence at the end of the first part of a song-form beginning in major will be a perfect authentic cadence in the key, or a heavy cadence in the key of the dominant; if beginning in minor, it will be an authentic cadence in the relative key.

The Two-part Song-form resembles and is hard to distinguish from the contrasting double period, the difference being that the cadence at the end of a part is heavier than that at the end of the first period. Many hymn-tunes and popular songs are written in this form.

In minor the 4th degree is raised in the $II_{2\#}^7$ and $IV_{1\#}^7$ chords.

The 4th degree is raised in conjunction with the 6th in the $II_{\#\natural}$, $II_{\#\natural}^7$, $IV_{\#\natural}$

and $IV_{\#\natural}^7$ chords.

Section A.

(1) Construct Two-part Song-forms in f minor, using all types of modulations to next related and remote keys. Use all embellishments, and employ the meter and rhythms given on page 297.

Section B.

(1) *Practise the following Chord Successions:*
   (a) Play the entire exercise, listening to the character of the chords and modulations.
   (b) Pause before each modulation and think the progression into the new key.
   (c) Sing the number-names of the soprano as you play the chords.
   (d) Have each exercise dictated as outlined on page 161.

(2) *Practise the following Intervals:*

    (a) Play the I, IV#♮, II#♮, V⁷ and I chords in the key of f minor. Think the sound of the intervals.

    (b) Play the intervals, determining their sound in relation to the root of the chords and the key-centre.

    (c) Sing the intervals.

    (d) Transpose the intervals to other minor keys.

(3)   *Exercises for Melodic Dictation:*

(a)   Play the I, IV$_\natural$, IV$^7_{\sharp\natural}$, II$^7_{1\natural}$, I$_2$, V^7 and I chords in the key of f minor. Read each exercise mentally, noting the modulations and embellishments.

(b)   Sing the last few notes in the key before the modulation, then the first few in the new key, first to *la*, thinking the number-names, then singing the number-names.

(c)   Play the antecedent phrase twice.   Sing from memory to *la*.   Sing mentally the number-names, then use the letter-names.   Sing both aloud.

(d)   Practise the other phrases in the same way.

(e)   Transpose to other minor keys.

(f)   Have each melody dictated as outlined on page 87.

Section C.

> (1) *Rhythmic Drill.* Irregular Rhythm in 12/8 meter.
>> (a) Practise using the arm movement to indicate the meter. Sing the rhythm to *la* on a major scale.

Largo

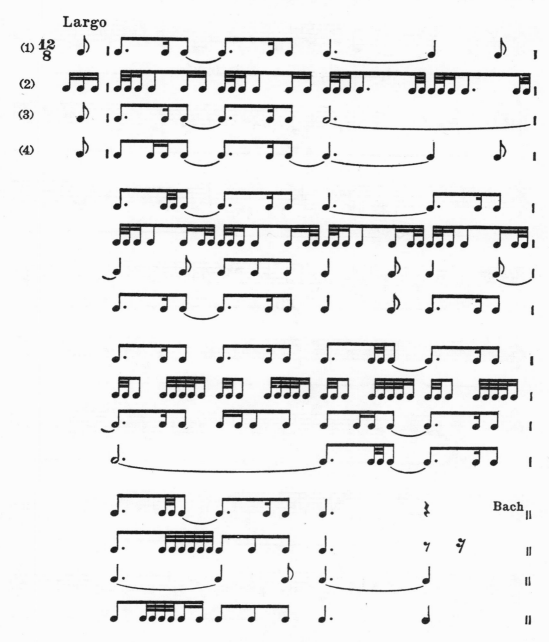

(2) *Practise the following Chord Successions:*
   (a) Sing each exercise mentally.
   (b) Sing the letter-, then the number-names.
   (c) Sing to *la*, thinking the number- and letter-names.
   (d) Sing from dictation.

(e) Sing the following chord successions, first by letter-, then by number-names, then to *la:* (1) I, $_0$V^9, I $_0$V$^9_\flat$,I $_0$V$^9_\flat$, I $_0$V$^9_\flat$ $_0$V^9 $_0$V^9, I

II$^7_2$, I$_2$, II$^7_{2\sharp\natural}$, V$^7_1$, I. (2) I, II$^7_3$, $_0$V^9, V$^7_1$, I $_0$V^9,I V^7 V^7 V^7

V^7 V^7, I, I$_1$ II$^7_{\sharp\natural}$, V$^7_1$, I.

(3) *Exercises for Sight-Singing:*

Bach

Schubert

LESSON 33

When three parts are used, the composition is known as a *Three-Part Song-Form.* In the Three-part Song-form the third part is always an exact or modified repetition of the first part. This is the most common construction in all art forms. The *aria da capo*, most songs and short piano pieces are written in this form. The cadence at the end of the first part is the same as in the two-part song-form; the cadence at the end of the second part is generally a perfect authentic cadence in the key of the dominant or dominant harmony in the key; the cadence at the end of the third part is a perfect authentic cadence in the key.

In minor the 2nd degree is lowered in the II♭, II♭⁷ and ₀V♭⁹ chords.

Section A.

(1) Construct Three-part Song-forms in c# minor, using all types of modulations to next related and remote keys. Use all embellishments, and employ the meter and rhythms given on page 307.

Section B.

(1) *Practise the following Chord Successions:*
- (a) Play the entire exercise, listening to the character of the chords and modulations.
- (b) Pause before each modulation and think the progression into the new key.
- (c) Sing the number-names of the soprano as you play the chords.
- (d) Have each exercise dictated as outlined on page 161.

(2) *Practise the following Intervals:*
(a) Play the I, IV, II$_{1b}$, V^7 and I chords in the key of c♯ minor. Think the sound of the intervals.
(b) Play the intervals, determining their sound in relation to the root of the chords and the key-centre.
(c) Sing the intervals.
(d) Transpose the intervals to other minor keys.

(3) *Exercises for Melodic Dictation:*
(a) Play the I, IV, II^1_b, I$_2$, V^7 and I chords in the key of c♯ minor. Read each exercise mentally, noting the modulations and embellishments.
(b) Sing the last few notes in the key before the modulation, then the first few in the new key, first to *la*, thinking the number-names, then singing the number-names.
(c) Play the antecedent phrase twice. Sing from memory to *la*. Sing mentally the number-names, then use the letter-names. Sing both aloud.
(d) Practise the other phrases in the same way.
(e) Transpose to other minor keys.
(f) Have each melody dictated as outlined on page 87.

Section C.

(1) *Rhythmic Drill.* Five Pulse Measure.

A five pulse meter is generally the result of combining a duple and a triple meter. The duple and triple measure are signified either by the beaming, by the slurs, or by dotted bars dividing the measure.

The Tschaikowsky example combines a duple and a triple measure. In 5 and 6 Debussy draws a dotted bar to show the division. In 7, Elgar shows the measure by the beaming.

Debussy

Elgar D. of G.

Voice part

(2) *Practise the following Chord Successions:*
(a) Sing each exercise mentally.
(b) Sing the letter-names, then use the number-names.
(c) Sing to *la*, thinking the number- and letter-names.
(d) Sing from dictation.

(e) Sing the following chord successions, first by letter-, then by number-names, then to *la:* (1) $I, II^7_{3,0}V^9, V^7_1, I$ V^7_1, I $II^7_{2\#}, I_2, II^7_{2\#\natural}, V^7_1, I$ [c# minor] [E maj.] [e minor]

$V, II^7_{2\#}, V^7_1, I$ V, V^7_3, I_1 V^7_1, I $V^7_1, I, II^7_{2\#}, I_2, IV^7_{1\#}, I_2, II^7_{2\#\natural}, V^7_1, I.$ [F major] [a minor] [d minor] [c# minor]

(2) $I, V^7_3, I_1, II^7, V^7_2, I$ V^7, I II^7_3, V^7_1, I V^7_3, I_1 V^7_1, I II^7_3, V^7_1, I [c# minor] [f# min.] [e minor] [A maj.] [d minor] [c minor]

$_0V^9, V^7_1, I, V^7_2, I_1, IV^7_\#, I_2, V^7_2, I.$ [c# minor]

(3) *Exercises for Sight-Singing:*

Tschaikowsky

Vidal

Hageman

INTERVALS

Lesson	Position				To sing as Unrelated	
	On Staff	In Major Scale	In Minor Scale	In Chords	Up	Down
Major 2nd	All but e-f, b-c	All but 3-4, 7-8	All but 2-3, 5-6, 7-8	All 7th Chords but the IV⁷, I⁷	1-2	5-4
Minor 2nd	E-f, b-c	3-4, 7-8	2-3, 5-6, 7-8	IV⁷ and I⁷	7-8	8-7
Major 3rd	From c, f & g	From 1, 4 & 5	From 3, 5 & 6	All Chords but the VII	1-3	3-1
Minor 3rd	From d, e, a & b	From 2, 3, 6 & 7	From 1, 2, 4 & 7	All Chords	3-5	5-3
Perfect 4th	All but f-b	All but 4-7	All but 4-7, 6-2, 7-3	All but VII	5-8	8-5
Perfect 5th	All but b-f	All but 7-4	All but 7-4, 2-6, 3-7	All but VII	1-5	5-1
Major 6th	From c, d, f & g	From 1, 2, 4 & 5	From 2, 3, 4 & 6	All Chords	5-3	3-5
Minor 6th	From e, a & b	From 3, 6 & 7	From 1, 5 & 7	All Chords but VII	3-8	8-3
Major 7th	From c & f	From 1 & 4	From 1, 3 & 6	IV⁷	1-7	7-1
Minor 7th	From d, e, g, a & b	From 2, 3, 5, 6 & 7	From 2, 4, 5 & 7	All 7th Chords but IV⁷, I⁷	5-4	8-2
Aug. 4th	From f-b	From 4-7, 1-#4, ♭6-2, 6-#2, 3-#6	From 4-7, 6-2, 1-#4, 3-♮6	V⁷, II⁷##, II⁷♭, ₀V♭⁵, VI⁷##	4-7	7-4
Dim. 5th	From b-f	From 7-4, #4-1, 2-♭6, #2-6, #6-3	From 7-4, 2-6, #4-8, ♮6-3		7-4	4-7
Dim. 7th		From 7-♭6, #2-8, #6-5	From 7-6, #4-3	₀V⁹, II⁷##, VI⁷##	Same as Major 6th	Same as Major 6th
Aug. 2nd		From ♭6-7, 8-#2, 5-#6	From 6-7, 3-#4		Minor 3rd	Minor 3rd
Aug 5th		From 5-#2	From 3-7	V# in Maj. III in Min.	Minor 6th	Minor 6th
Dim. 4th		From #2-5	From 7-3		Major 3rd	Major 3rd
Minor 9th		From 5-♭6	From 5-6	V⁹♭	Minor 2nd	Minor 2nd
Aug. 6th		From ♭6-#4, ♭2-7, 4-#2	From 6-#4, ♭2-7	II⁷##♭, V♭⁷, V⁷#	Minor 7th	Minor 7th
Dim. 3rd		From #4-♭6, 7-♭8, #2-4	From #4-6, 7-♭2		Major 2nd	Major 2nd
Double Dim. 5th		From #2-♭6		II⁷##♭, V⁹#♭	Per. 4th	Per. 4th
Double Aug. 4th		From ♭6-#2			Per. 5th	Per. 5th

Keyboard Harmony

A Practical Application of Music Theory Including the Study of Melody Harmonization, Broken Chords and Arpeggios, Transposition, Modulation and Improvisation

By GEORGE A. WEDGE

MUSIC THEORY is a study which has become essential to the fully equipped musician, and which, in consequence, most pupils take up as a part of their proper musical education. It is generally followed as a separate subject from the pupil's chosen instrument or particular field; very few realize its far-reaching application and value.

This book is an endeavor to show the teachers and pupils of piano how to apply, at the keyboard, each theoretic point and to give exercises for practice.

Price, $3.00
(In U. S. A.)

G. Schirmer, Inc.

609 Fifth Avenue,   New York 17, N. Y.

A 686